Jack Youll VC
Great War Hero

Other Titles by Paul Chrystal and in print with Pen & Sword Books

A History of Chocolate in York (2012)
Roman Military Disasters: Dark Days and Lost Legions (2015)
Women at War in the Classical World (2017)
Leeds's Military Legacy (2017)
Emperors of Rome: The Monsters – From Tiberius to Theodora, AD 14–548 (2018)
British Army of the Rhine: The BAOR, 1945–1993 (2018)
Rome: Republic into Empire – The Civil Wars of the First Century BCE (2019)
War in Roman Myth and Legend (2020)
War in Greek Mythology (2020)
A Historical Guide to Roman York (2021)
The History of Sweets (2021)
The History of the World in 100 Pandemics, Plagues and Epidemics (2021)
Rowntree's – The Early History (2021)
Factory Girls: The Working Lives of Women and Children (2022)
Bioterrorism and Biological Warfare: Disease as a Weapon of War (2023)
Gunners from the Sky: 1st Air Landing Light Regiment in Italy and at Arnhem, 1942–44 (2024)
Women at Work in World Wars I and II: Factories, Farms and the Military and Civil Services (2024)
World-Changing Women: 150 Women who Rewrote the Histories of Ancient Egypt, Israel, Greece and Rome (2024)
The Seaforth Highlanders: Aiding the King, 1881–1961 (2025)
The Book in the Ancient World: How the Wisdom of the Ages Was Preserved (2025)

For a full list please go to www.paulchrystal.com

Jack Youll VC Great War Hero

And the First World War on the Western Front and in Italy

Paul Chrystal and Nina Youll

Pen & Sword
MILITARY

First published in Great Britain in 2025 by
Pen & Sword Military
An imprint of Pen & Sword Books Limited
Yorkshire – Philadelphia

Copyright © Paul Chrystal and Nina Youll 2025

ISBN 978 1 03610 897 7

The rights of Paul Chrystal and Nina Youll to be identified as Authors of this Work has been asserted by them in accordance with the Copyright, Designs and Patents Act 1988.

A CIP catalogue record for this book is available from the British Library.

All rights reserved. No part of this book may be reproduced, transmitted, downloaded, decompiled or reverse engineered in any form or by any means, electronic or mechanical including photocopying, recording or by any information storage and retrieval system, without permission from the Publisher in writing. NO AI TRAINING: Without in any way limiting the Author's and Publisher's exclusive rights under copyright, any use of this publication to 'train' generative artificial intelligence (AI) technologies to generate text is expressly prohibited. The Author and Publisher reserve all rights to license uses of this work for generative AI training and development of machine learning language models.

Typeset by Mac Style
Printed in the UK by CPI Group (UK) Ltd, Croydon, CR0 4YY.

The Publisher's authorised representative in the EU for product safety is Authorised Rep Compliance Ltd., Ground Floor, 71 Lower Baggot Street, Dublin D02 P593, Ireland.
www.arccompliance.com

For a complete list of Pen & Sword titles please contact

PEN & SWORD BOOKS LIMITED
47 Church Street, Barnsley, South Yorkshire, S70 2AS, England
E-mail: enquiries@pen-and-sword.co.uk
Website: www.pen-and-sword.co.uk
or
PEN AND SWORD BOOKS
1950 Lawrence Road, Havertown, PA 19083, USA
E-mail: uspen-and-sword@casematepublishers.com
Website: www.penandswordbooks.com

The Royal Northumberland Fusiliers, one of the toughest infantry regiments the army has ever mustered

John McManners in Allan Mallinson's
*The Making of the British Army:
from the English Civil War to the War on Terror* (2009)

Contents

About the Authors		ix
Acknowledgements		x
List of Illustrations		xii
Maps		xiv
Preface		xviii
Introduction		xxi
Chapter 1	Jack Youll (1897–1918) – His Early Life in Thornley, Co. Durham	1
Chapter 2	Jack Youll and the 1st Durham Engineers	18
Chapter 3	A Very Short History of The Northumberland Fusiliers 1674–1918	21
Chapter 4	11th Northumberland Fusiliers in France	28
Chapter 5	11th Northumberland Fusiliers Regimental War Diaries and Orders	32
Chapter 6	11th Northumberland Fusiliers: Hill 60 (Ypres) and the Battle of Messines	45
Chapter 7	11th Northumberland Fusiliers in Italy and the British Expeditionary Force (Italy)	56
Chapter 8	The Battle of Asiago, 15–23 June	74
Chapter 9	Jack Youll's VC Action	84

Chapter 10	The Hero Returns to Thornley, 10 September 1918	89
Chapter 11	Ernest Hemingway and Edward Brittain in Asiago	92
Chapter 12	Jack Youll Killed in Action at the Battle of Vittorio Veneto, October 1918	105
Chapter 13	Lord Ashcroft's Hero of the Month	117
Chapter 14	Thomas Kenny VC, W. McNally VC and W. Wood VC	118

Timeline for Jack Youll VC (1897–1918) 138
Appendix 1: The German Bombardment of Hartlepool & West Hartlepool 141
Appendix 2: Other Memorials to Jack Youll 143
Appendix 3: Structure of the British Army During The First World War 144
Appendix 4: First World War Casualties by Nation 146
Notes 148
Further Reading 160
Index 163

About the Authors

Paul Chrystal attended the universities of Hull and Southampton where he studied classics (BA Hons and MPhil), and Sorbonne University, Paris; then for the next 35 years he worked in medical publishing sales.

More recently he has been history advisor to various Yorkshire visitor attractions, writing features for national newspapers, and broadcasting on radio, including BBC Sounds, Radio 4's 'PM' programme and on the BBC World Service. He has done numerous presentations and book signings/launches, as well as frequent webinars.

Paul is the author of over 180 books on a wide range of subjects. He is past editor of *York Historian*, journal of the Yorkshire Architectural and York Archaeological Society, and of *Yorkshire Archaeological Journal*.

Nina Youll is a First Class BA (Hons) Spanish and English Language graduate of York St John University; she is a CELTA qualified (Pass B) English as a foreign/second language teacher. Since June 2023 she has been an International Student Mobility Assistant at Teesside University. Before that she was International Development Manager at YSJ University where she represented the university internationally, to raise awareness of the brand in pursuit of international student recruitment targets and contribute to diversifying the international student body at both YSJ York and London campuses. The role involved promoting undergraduate and postgraduate degrees, short courses, summer schools, identifying opportunities for Transnational Education (TNE) and online learning. Working with the Head of International Development, she focussed on the European and Sri Lankan markets. Nina first learnt about Jack Youll when the family began researching their family history only to discover a significant local tribute to Jack in Thornaby, which is where the family originally came from before relocating to Hartlepool. Although the details were a little lost among generations of Johns (Jacks), Nina's grandfather (William Youll) always took great pride in knowing they were connected, however distantly, to a Victoria Cross recipient.

Acknowledgements

No book is ever the work of one man or woman; it usually depends on the help and advice provided by other authors, librarians and archivists, friends and family.

So, my thanks go out to Nina Youll, my co-author, who provided the inspiration and idea for this book and information on Jack Youll's family history; to Margaret Hedley of Wheatley Hill History Club (wheatley-hill.org.uk) who gave much valuable and hard-to-find detail; likewise Lesley Frater, Museum Manager, Fusiliers Museum of Northumberland, Alnwick Castle for being so extraordinarily helpful in allowing access to and photographing for me many hard-to-access exhibits relating to Jack Youll both in the museum and in the archives. Thanks also go to Julian Harrop, Collections Resources Co-ordinator at Beamish Museum for permission to use the three images of Thornley from the People's Collection Archive. To prove that the fighting never really stops, the Quality Manager at the National Archives in Kew was very helpful despite the fact that many of his records, including Jack Youll's, were burnt to a cinder by Luftwaffe bombing in September 1940 when Germany and Britain resumed hostilities and the War Office repository in Arnside Street took a direct hit. Chris Baker, author of 'The Long, Long Trail' website on the British Army in the Great War, and former chairman of the Western Front Association has been kind enough to allow me to use extracts from his encyclopaedic body of work, particularly in relation to Jack at the Battle of Asiago Plateau, based on the war diaries of the various divisions, along with a mixture of divisional and regimental histories; his invaluable website is at https://www.fourteeneighteen.co.uk/chris-baker/

I must thank the compilers and editors of a handful of magnificent books which have assisted me enormously. First is *The Employees and Residents of Thornley, Ludworth & Wheatley Hill: Their Contribution in the Great War 1914–1918*. Those compilers have painstakingly and as exhaustively as possible trawled through local records and badgered local residents to bring together an invaluable primary resource which achieves its aim of honouring those soldiers from the area who served on one or other of the battle fronts. Full of personal photographs, newspaper cuttings and documents, its 223 large format pages provide the researcher with a tour de force in First World War studies. The compilers are Fred Bromilow, Owen Roland, John Burrell and Graham Stewart.

Second is Norman Gladden's *Across the Piave 1917–1919* – his informative personal account of the British forces in Italy sheds light on much of what Jack Youll must have experienced, since they both served in the same battalion of the Northumberland Fusiliers in the Italian theatre.

The third is Tony Ball's *Crossing No Man's Land* – another triumph of primary research – which provides, in granular detail, the Northumberland Fusilier way of prosecuting a war: battalion by battalion, battle by battle, day by day. And, as our largest infantry regiment in the Great War, they should know. All of this is based on Tony Ball's painstaking reading and analysis of all 'two-hundred and eleven attacks and 75 raids [as] identified through a census of all 28 of the Regiment's battalion war diaries covering 28,876 diary days'. The 211 attacks took place on 201 days. From this we establish what each battalion, including Jack Youll's 11th, 'was engaged in every day and for the Regiment in aggregate'. Indeed, as Tony Ball states in his Preface: 'If you know your Fusilier's Battalion number and when he served then the data in the appendices will allow you to construct a personalised activity and battle profile'. We do and we have. Follow that.

Finally, I must record what an honour and privilege it has been to research and write the story of Jack Youll; from the evidence I have sourced I can say it would be hard to 'meet' a braver, more selfless and self-effacing man.

List of Illustrations

Jack Youll VC. (*Republished in* Victoria Cross Heroes of World War One *by Robert Hamilton (2015, Atlantic Publishing) from the archives of Associated Newspapers*)
Thornley Colliery clearly showing how the pit dominates the village.
The Villas, the street where Jack grew up.
The Workmen's Club, Thornley.
Jack's school: the County Council School.
The gardens surrounding the Jack Youll Memorial in Thornley today.
The Jack Youll Memorial.
Gallantry information found on the Jack Youll Memorial.
The first stanza from Rupert Brooke's *The Dead* poignantly marking Jack Youll's death. *The Dead* is part of English poet Rupert Brooke's sequence '1914': five linked poems that honoured the fallen soldiers of the First World War. In this sonnet, a speaker laments all the small joys of life that the dead must leave behind but finds consolation in the thought that death also offers a 'shining peace' in which the fallen can rest. Brooke published the poem in his 1915 collection *1914 and Other Poems*. (*Courtesy of Fusiliers Museum of Northumberland https://www.northumberlandfusiliers.org.uk/*)
Smashed up German trench with corpses after the Battle of Messines Ridge. (*National Library of Scotland/public domain*)
Carnage on Hill 60.
A jubilant group of Northumberland Fusiliers enjoying life with captured German gas masks and helmets after the Battle of St Eloi Craters, 27 March–16 April 1916, Ypres Salient. (*NAM 1998-06-181-7*)

List of Illustrations   xiii

Troops of the 1/5th Battalion, Northumberland Fusiliers waiting their turn for a haircut, Toutencourt, October 1916. Note that the second man in the queue is wearing a German cap. (*IWM Q1366*)

Italian troops salvaging what they can after a trench takes a direct hit.

Fighting high up in the mountains.

Newspaper cutting citing Jack Youll's brave action at Polygon Wood, which won him a mention in despatches. (The Graphic, *27 July 1918 – www.ukphotoarchive.org.uk/the-graphic-portraits-xyz/h75719F22#h75719f22*)

The watch presented to Jack Youll by the people of Thornley. (*Courtesy of Fusiliers Museum of Northumberland*)

Second Lieutenant Jack Youll VC.

A proud Jack Youll showing off his VC to a comrade. (*https://www.ukphotoarchive.org.uk/ww1victoriacrossrecipients/h814671A8#h814671a8*)

The cigarette case presented to Jack Youll by the people of Thornley. (*Courtesy of Fusiliers Museum of Northumberland*)

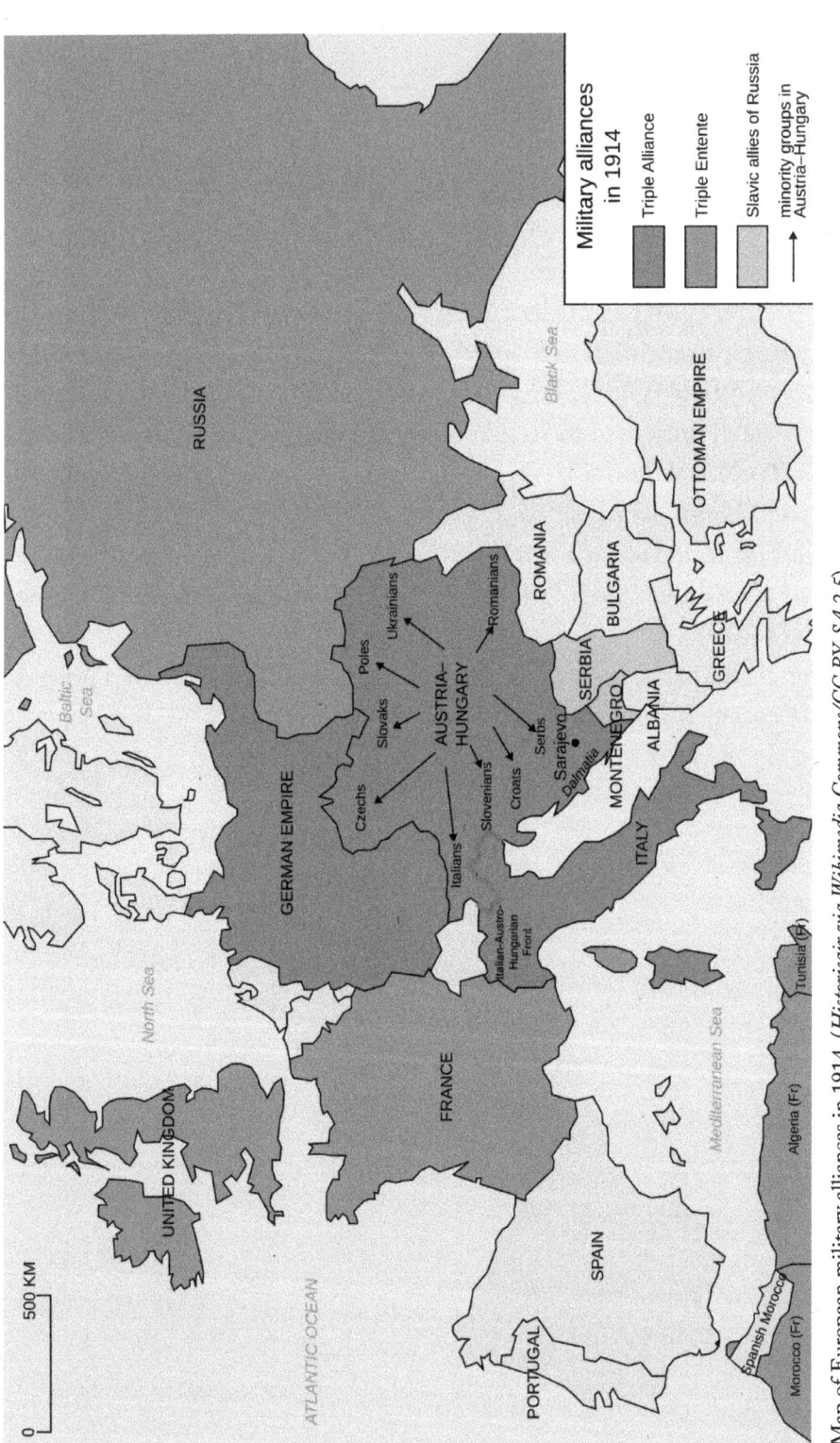

Map of European military alliances in 1914. (*Historicair via Wikimedia Commons/CC BY-SA 2.5*)

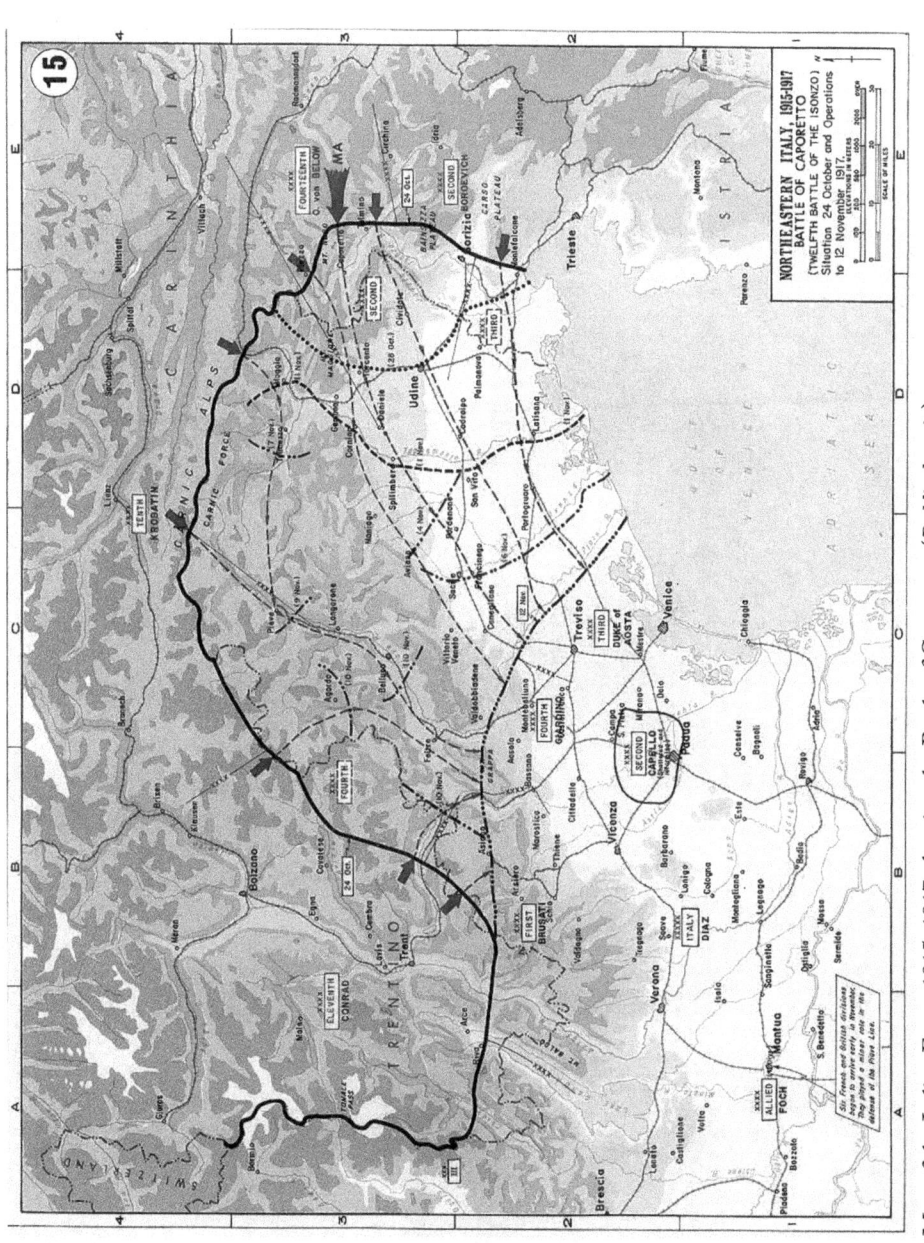

Map of the Italian Front, 1915–1917, showing the Battle of Caporetto. (*Public domain*)

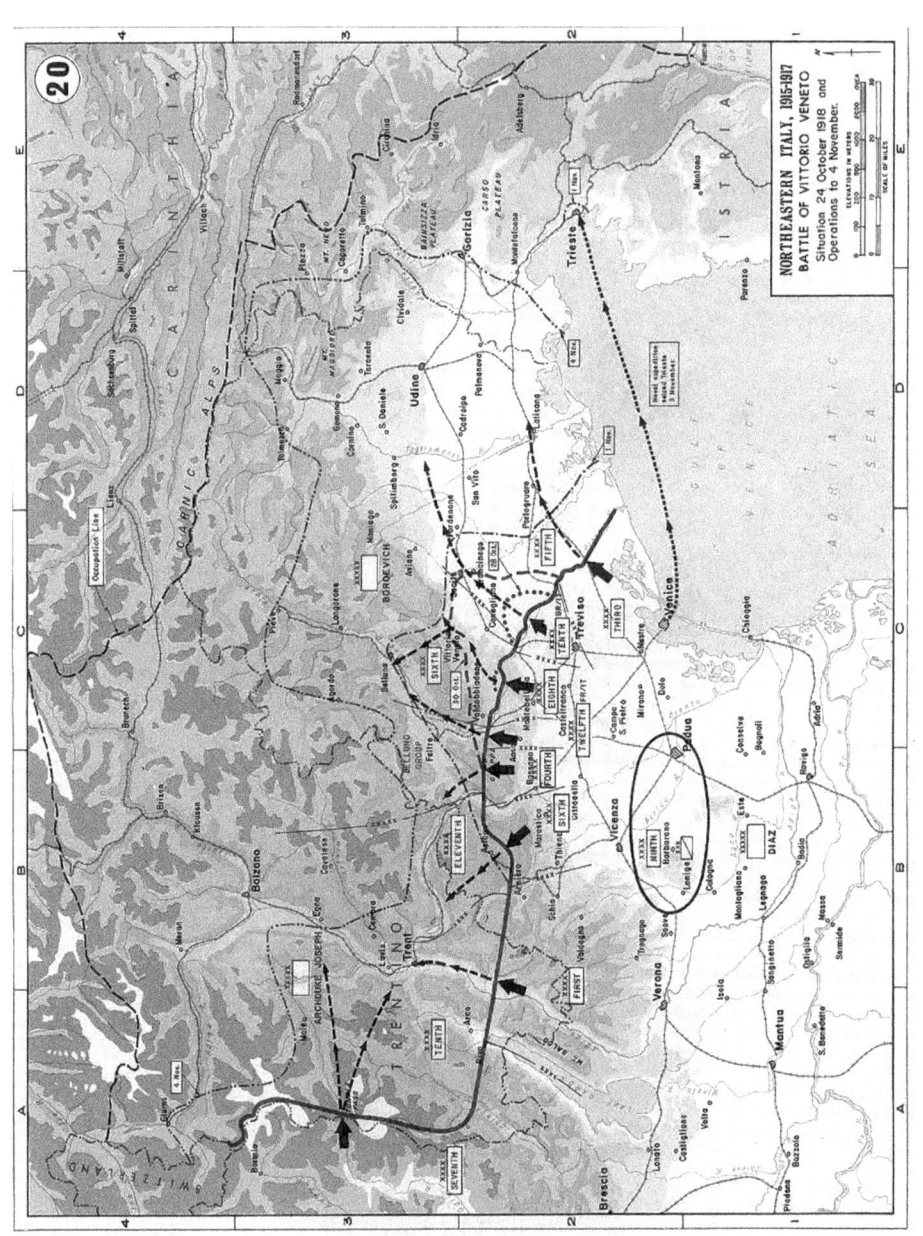

Map of the Battle of Vittorio Veneto. (*Public domain*)

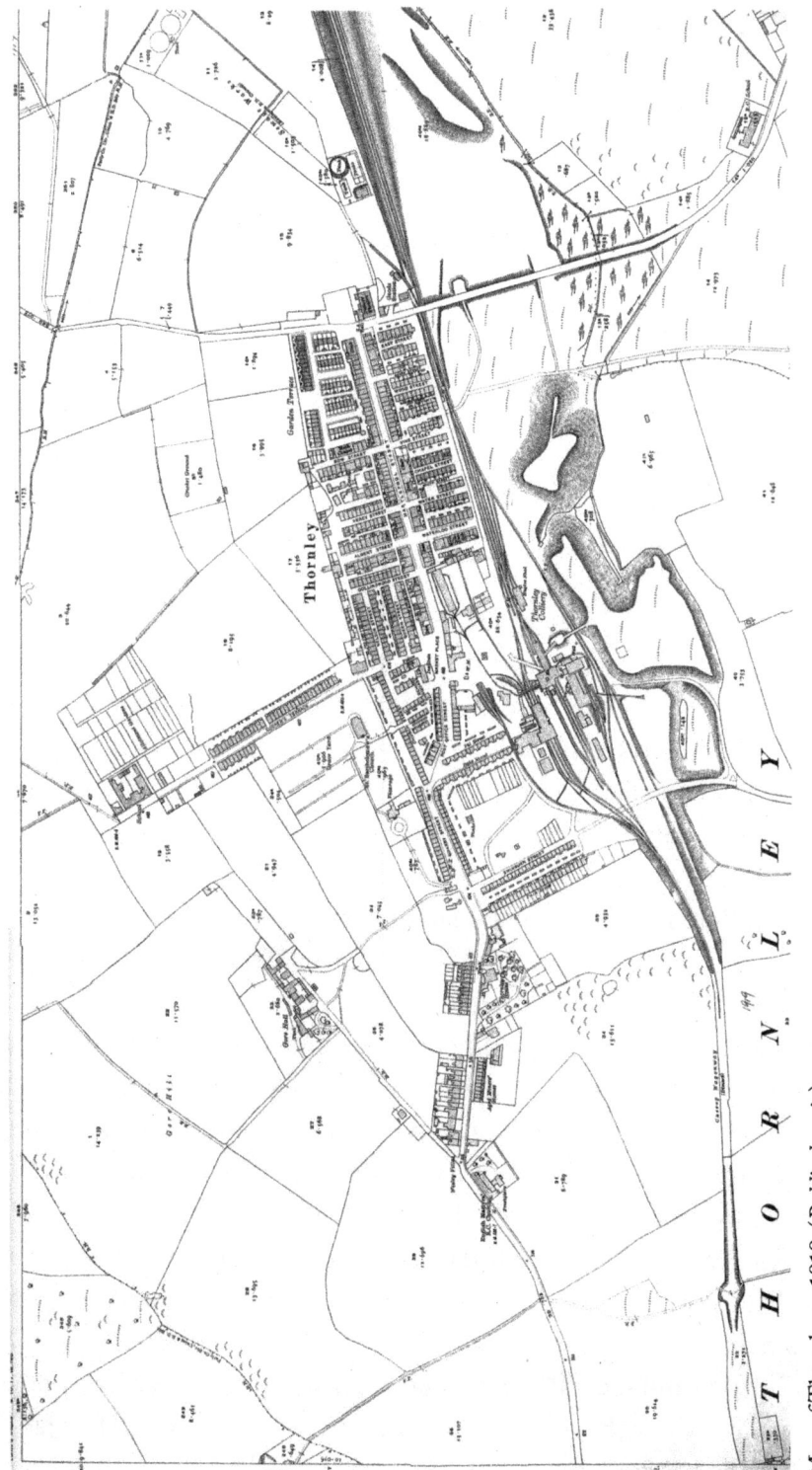

Map of Thornley c. 1919. (*Public domain*)

Preface

John Scott Youll VC (6 June 1897–27 October 1918) was awarded the Victoria Cross for a truly magnanimous and courageous action which took place on 15 June 1918, just south west of Asiago in the Veneto region of Italy.

Comparatively speaking, until now not that much has been written to celebrate Jack Youll's outstanding deeds, so there is consequently little to remind us of his bravery, save listings often duplicated in various books describing VC winners in general. But most importantly, a dignified memorial was erected in 2005 in his home colliery village of Thornley, west of Hartlepool in County Durham.

This book puts right the shortage of information relating to Jack Youll in the literature with the first detailed account of his short life, his time in the 11th Battalion, Northumberland Fusiliers (Britain's largest infantry unit in the Great War) and a full account of his bravery at Asiago. It concludes with his tragic death, just days before the Italian armistice, and with his legacy as a local hero – a credit to Thornley, to County Durham, to Britain and to the British Army. He had been posted from the Western Front when Britain and France responded to Italy's call for Allied support to combat the Austrians in the north of Italy. In 1914 Italy was neutral but joined the Entente in 1915.[1]

Tragically, Jack Youll was killed in action at the Battle of Vittoria Veneto in which the Italian Army and its allies launched a decisive and successful counter-offensive against the forces of the Austro-Hungarian Empire (1867–1918) and their allies; the victory significantly marked the end of the war in Italy with an armistice a mere twenty-four hours after Jack's death – and the end of the First World War itself one short week later.[2]

The pivotal Battle of Vittoria Veneto had massive far-reaching and global significance: it sealed the fate of the once mighty Austro-Hungarian Empire. At the other end of the historical and political spectrum, back in Thornley Jack's family were notified of his death on 10 November 1918, the day before the Armistice was signed.

Nina Youll is a near-relative of Jack Youll and has provided information and details, much of which has hitherto been unseen by the reading public for over 100 years.

In writing the book we have been careful throughout to put Jack's short life into context, both locally and globally. Jack, like us all, did not live in a bubble, immune from external influences; his actions did not take place in a vacuum. His life journey was determined by incidents and coincidences which led him in one direction or another. So, we describe his early life in Thornley, and the impact the mining community and his family might have had on him there, and on major decisions taken later in life; we describe local and international events leading up to the beginning of the Great War which may have influenced an ambition to join up; we describe that life-changing assassination in Sarajevo which triggered it all; we trace Jack's combat experiences on the Western Front and early signs of selfless bravery with his mention in despatches at Polygon Wood; we look at the experiences of others in the same battles he fought and we scrutinise the war diaries which narrate the trench life he and his comrades in the same or other battalions of the Northumberland Fusiliers went through. We explain how Italy changed sides when they saw which way the winds of war were blowing, leading ultimately to Jack's posting to northern Italy, his VC, his Italian silver medal and his tragic death within an ace of surviving the war. We contextualise this with the experiences of three writers who help us by directly or indirectly describing their personal experiences in that same theatre of war, so shedding light on what Jack and his comrades were up against on that northern Italian front line: Ernest Hemingway, Edward Brittain and Norman Gladden.

Finally, we close the book with more context, this time through descriptions of three other VCs won by Northumberland Fusiliers in the First World War: Thomas Kenny VC, W. McNally VC and W. Wood VC. Kenny and McNally were born and grew up very near Jack Youll in County Durham.

Introduction

The Great War

How did the First World War happen? What were the causes of this 'war to end all wars', this war which in 1914 was confidently expected 'to end before Christmas' with the allies occupying Berlin?

The turn of the twentieth century began with the Industrial Revolution (1760–1840) and German unification (1866–1871, *Deutsche Einigung*) behind us (but not the various impacts they made) with Britain, France, Belgium, Germany and Italy busy expanding their colonies and empires in their often rapacious scrambles for Africa and other vulnerable countries beyond Europe's borders.

As Michael Howard points out in his *The First World War, A Very Short Introduction*, p. 2):[1]

> 'Britain had led the way ... she was already a fully urbanised and industrial nation but the last vestiges of political power were being wrested from it by a House of Commons in which the two major parties competed for the vote, not just of the middle, but increasingly, as the franchise was extended, of the working classes.'

The major problem though for Britain was an existentialist one. Developed as we were with all the affluence and power which accrued from the largest empire in the world, the rubies and silks only percolated down to a very small minority of traders, financiers and property owners. And for that to happen, we, as an island nation, relied entirely on trade to keep us fed and allow us to thrive. The jaunty, jingoistic 'Rule, Britannia! Britannia rule the waves ...' had been written in 1740, but its message was just as affirming 180 years later: God forbid we lost the naval supremacy which ensured our lifeblood, kept us on the world stage and allowed us to police and subdue our extensive empire. This understandable anxiety quite naturally informed Britain's policies towards its neighbours and international competitors.

The Germans, in the meantime, viewed any alliance between France and Russia, and Britain's supremacy over the waves of the German Ocean with some concern: but from 1891 the two powers regardless signed agreements, the Dual Entente or Franco-Russian Alliance, to counterbalance the Triple Alliance of Germany, Austria-Hungary, and Italy. Britain, then, had some bridges to build and so differences between France and Britain over Africa were resolved in 1904 (*l'entente cordiale*). In 1907 border disputes over Persia and Afghanistan with a Russian Empire weakened by war with Japan were concluded, allowing Britain to join France and Russia in the 'Triple Entente'.[2]

All the while the Germans were building up their fleet, as were the increasingly edgy British; an early demonstration of Germany's success here came in December 1914 when three battle cruisers of the German Imperial Navy bombarded with virtual impunity the north-east towns of Hartlepool, West Hartlepool, Whitby and Scarborough, causing death and destruction on a huge scale while the hapless Royal Navy lost the Germans in the fog and Churchill was taking a bath in Whitehall. It is unlikely that a teenage Jack Youll would not have heard all about such an outrage in his mining village a few miles to the west, and that he was not affected by the patriotism, anti-German loathing and anger no doubt felt by his friends and the men and women of Thornley and its neighbourhood.

The only silver lining to the murderous shelling was that the outrage stimulated the British recruitment campaign beyond all expectation; at the same time it fuelled an anti-German sentiment that had been simmering since Britain's movement towards France, and Germany's cynical baiting in 1911 of the French by demonstrating their superiority with a show of force off Agadir in Morocco.[3] France was, to the average Briton, the ally of choice whereas Germany was becoming the enemy to beat if or when it came to war.

Archduke Franz Ferdinand, Gavrilo Princip and the July Crisis

Serbia was a problem. After years of turmoil and two Balkan Wars, the Serbs came out triumphant, assisted ably by their covert terrorist unit, the Black Hand, trained and fed intelligence by the Serbian army. The Serbian population and its territory doubled in size, striking tremulous fear in the hearts of the Austrian government.

Then on 28 June 1914 Gavrilo Princip changed world history with two well-aimed pistol shots. He it was who at about 10.45 am assassinated Archduke Franz Ferdinand, heir presumptive to the Habsburg throne, and his wife, German-born Sophie, Duchess von Hohenberg, in Sarajevo, capital city of Bosnia-Herzegovina. Princip was a 19-year-old Bosnian Serb student terrorist in the pay of the Black Hand. His bullets were the first two of millions to follow which consigned 40 million more men, children and woman to an early death in the four years that followed.

This triggered the July Crisis, a series of events, miscalculations and naked national self-interest that within a month led to the outbreak of The Great War. Unfortunately for all concerned, the July Crisis turned out to be a political comedy of errors: a spider's web of Byzantine complexity in which hasty alliances, interlaced with the mistakes and misjudgements of numerous self-interested or ignorant (or both) political and military leaders (some who saw a war as being in their best interests, or believed that war was not a possibility), resulted in that lethal outbreak of hostilities amongst most of the major European states by early August 1914 as they indulged themselves in their high level squabbles.

Earlier on the fateful morning of 28 June 1914 the royal couple had, astonishingly, been attacked by Nedeljko Čabrinović, also a Young Bosnia conspirator, who had lobbed a grenade at their car. However, the device tumbled to the road and detonated behind them, injuring the occupants in the car following. This major security incident, however, failed to curtail or modify the official peacocking. On arriving at their destination, the Governor's residence, Franz exclaimed, not without some humour: 'So you welcome your guests with bombs!' With hindsight this ranks as one of the great breakdowns of security in history, ranking with the assassination of Julius Caesar in 44 BC, the attempted assassination of Adolf Hitler in the 20 July plot in 1944, and the assassinations of John and Robert F. Kennedy and Martin Luther King in the 1960s. The four security failures each changed the course of human history in less than half a minute.

The royal couple charitably insisted on visiting all those who had been injured by the grenade at the local hospital. However, there was a fateful breakdown in communication regarding a revised itinerary, and the Archduke's car ended up in a side street, stalled opposite Princip who was sitting at a cafe across the road. The terrorist saw his chance, crossed the street and shot the royal couple, Sophie first in the abdomen, and then Franz Ferdinand in the neck. Franz's dying words to Sophie were, 'Don't die darling, live for our children.'

Princip's weapon was the pocket-sized FN Model 1910 pistol chambered for the .380 ACP cartridge provided him by Serbian Army Military Intelligence Lieutenant Colonel and Black Hand leader Dragutin Dimitrijević. Franz Ferdinand died within minutes, while Sophie died on the way to the hospital.

Joachim Remak gives a vivid account of the assassination in *Sarajevo*:[4]

'One bullet pierced Franz Ferdinand's neck while the other pierced Sophie's abdomen…. As the car was reversing (to go back to the Governor's residence because the entourage thought the Imperial couple were unhurt) a thin streak of blood shot from the Archduke's mouth on to Count Harrach's right cheek (he was standing on the car's running board). Harrach drew out a handkerchief to still the gushing blood. The Duchess, seeing this, called: "For Heaven's sake! What happened to you?" and sank from her seat …

'Harrach and Potoriek …thought she had fainted …only her husband seemed to have an instinct for what was happening. Turning to his wife despite the bullet in his neck, Franz Ferdinand pleaded: "*Sopherl! Sopherl! Sterbe nicht! Bleibe am Leben für unsere Kinder!*" – "Sophie dear! Don't die! Stay alive for our children!" Having said this, he seemed to sag down himself. His plumed hat …fell off; many of its green feathers were found all over the car floor. Count Harrach seized the Archduke by the uniform collar to hold him up. He asked "*Leiden Eure Kaiserliche Hoheit sehr?*" – "Is Your Imperial Highness suffering very badly?" "*Es ist nichts.*" – "It is nothing." said the Archduke in a weak but audible voice. He seemed to be losing consciousness during his last few minutes, but, his voice growing steadily weaker, he repeated the phrase perhaps six or seven times more.

'A rattle began to issue from his throat, which subsided as the car drew in front of the Konak bersibin (Town Hall). Despite several doctors' efforts, the Archduke died shortly after being carried into the building while his beloved wife was almost certainly dead from internal bleeding before the motorcade reached the Konak.'

The assassination of Franz Ferdinand was certainly the most immediate cause of the First World War but there were many other contributing factors: subsequent assassinations, the arms race, nationalism, imperialism, increasing militarism of Imperial Germany, and the alliance system – none of these helped and led the world inexorably to the carnage and terror of the First World War, which began a month after Franz Ferdinand's death, with Austria-Hungary's declaration of war against Serbia – Vienna exploiting the situation to the full, using the assassination as the perfect pretext to take action against Serbia and seeing Serbia's nationalist aspirations as a threat to its own multi-ethnic empire. Austria-Hungary duly declared war on Serbia, closely followed by declarations of war by Germany, France, Russia and Great Britain.

After Franz Ferdinand's death, Archduke Karl Ludwig of Austria (1918–2007) became the heir presumptive of Austria-Hungary. Franz Ferdinand was buried with Sophie in Artstetten Castle, Austria.

It seems that Princip intended to fire a third shot but his weapon was torn from his hand before he was bundled to the ground where he succeeded in swallowing a capsule of cyanide – but this, for some reason, failed to kill him.[5] His trial ran from 12 October to 23 October, where Princip and twenty-four other alleged collaborators were indicted. The state charged twenty-two of the twenty-four with high treason and murder and the remaining three with conspiracy to murder.

The Black Hand was implicated in the assassination because it provided the weapons to the assassins and helped them cross the border. Although this did not prove that the Serbian government knew about the assassination, let alone approved of it, it was enough for Austria-Hungary to issue a démarche[6] to Serbia known as the July Ultimatum on 23 July, which led inexorably to the outbreak of the First World War.[7]

Princip was nineteen-years-old at the time and too young to be executed, being twenty-seven days short of the twenty-year minimum age limit required by Habsburg law for execution. On 28 October the court found Princip guilty of murder and high treason, for which he received the maximum sentence of twenty years in prison which he was to serve in a military prison ensconced within the Habsburg fortress of Theresienstadt in northern Bohemia (modern Czech Republic).

And so Princip was chained to a wall in solitary confinement at the Small Fortress there, where the harsh conditions he endured led to him developing tuberculosis.

Princip died on 28 April 1918, three years and ten months after the assassination, and while the Great War was still raging and the casualties on all sides continued to build ever higher. At the time of his death, weakened by malnutrition and co-morbidities, he weighed around 6st 4lb.

There is more astonishment when we realise that it happens that this assassination was, at the time, not seen as anything particularly world changing. There had been six or so serious terrorist incidents in the region since 1908, and these had all been peacefully resolved between the Allied Powers and the Central Powers.[8]

Crucially, though, Germany, seeing its chance, now pledged support for Austria in the event of war: to Berlin war was now an inevitability. At the same time Britain was never going to stand by and see France crushed by a Germany which now saw Britain as the only stumbling block in its ambition to become, not just the major power in Europe, but a world power.

4 August saw Germany flex her expansionist muscle when she illegally invaded neutral Belgium. Britain had an obligation to defend Belgium reaching back to the 1839 Treaty of London, which had guaranteed Belgium's independence and neutrality and was signed by all the major European powers, including Great Britain and Prussia. In 1914 Germany violated the treaty, using Belgium as a gateway into France.

Italy

How did Italy end up on the side of the Allies, the Entente, in May 1915, when they had signed up as a founding member of the Triple Alliance back in 1882 to collaborate with Austria and Germany? As Robert Hamilton says,[9] it was all 'rooted in 'self-interest' – nothing unusual you might say in a global conflict – but Italy's prime minister Antonio Salandra was an incurable opportunist and he only wanted to see what was best for Italy; so he weighed up the options and came to the conclusion that tearing up treaty obligations was a fair price to pay if it led to Italy's repossession of Austrian-held land harbouring a significant Italian population – and that at relatively low cost. While Salandra's parliament was a little hesitant, the Allies were only too enthusiastic to have gained a new ally hovering menacingly on Austria-Hungary's threshold.

Luigi Cadorna (1850–1928) was the general tasked with battling it out along the 400-mile craggy, hostile and unforgiving frontier; indeed, so hostile was it that by the end of 1916 progress was insignificant. Cadorna's objective was the port of Trieste, which involved crossing the

Isonzo River; nine battles ensued, none of them conclusive and all the while the soldiery was diminishing, as was its patience.

Hamilton tells us:

> 'The Austrians were in scarcely better fettle. New emperor Karl I was desperate to bring peace to his creaking domain. Erich Ludendorff, equally desperate to breathe life into the Austrian corpse, to which the Fatherland was shackled, recognised that German troops had to be deployed to break the deadlock. With Russia out of the war and the Tsar toppled, resources were available … ahead of the latest battle in October 1917 eight German divisions bolstered the Austrian attack, many of them specialists in Alpine combat. The result was emphatic. The last vestiges of the Italian army crumbled in a hail of gas shells, against which the troops had little protection. Thousands surrendered … Cadorna and the rump of his disintegrating army had no choice but to retreat. Austria took possession of Caporetto, the town that gave the Twelfth Battle of Asonzo, its popular name.'

A sixty-mile withdrawal to the River Piave did nothing to restore the confidence of Italy's allies. Diaz replaced the mercurial and much loathed Cadorna, a shortage of food amongst the Austrians helped restore some calm. The Battle of the Piave followed, in which two of the six VCs of the whole Italian campaign were awarded.

What sort of war was it for an infantryman?

So Britain embarked on a war which, it is safe to say, they had no real idea from the outset how to prosecute, how to supply or how to man. Nevertheless, by the armistice in 1918, 5,704,416 men and women had served or were still serving. The Great War has been termed the first industrial war, with the first significant use of tanks and the deployment of chemical and biological warfare, both of which had been with us as early as the fifth century BC in the hands of the belligerent ancient

Greeks, but honed now for greater impact with gas and flamethrowers (*flammenwerfer* to the Germans).[10]

Comparatively speaking, the infantryman was not just a vulnerable soldier, he was a busy vulnerable soldier. Infantry averaged 1,581,649 men over the course of the war and between them they participated in 81 battles, 55 of which were offensive or attacking while the remaining 26 were defensive. Jack Youll was embroiled in five of these from summer 1917 to autumn 1918, all offensive bar one. The Battalion total of battles from 1916 to 1918 was nine.

Trenches

If anything characterised the nature of the Great War it was the wretched trench (known formally as 'position warfare'), especially on the Western Front, which was used to good effect by both adversaries and was in effect their front lines; the bit in the middle was the much coveted no-man's-land.

Trench warfare started with the Crimean War (1853–1856) and was used in the American Civil War (1861–1865) and the Russo-Japanese War (1904–1905). Ball (2016, p. 35) tells us that:

> 'Improvements to both small arms and artillery technology throughout the 19th century had resulted in greater volumes of fire and increased range and accuracy which had made movement in the open within range of the enemy an extremely hazardous activity. Entrenching or digging in was an obvious response'.

Life Expectancy and Casualties

When Jack Youll signed up with the Northumberland Fusiliers he was joining an infantry regiment and thus was four times more likely to be killed in action than an engineer, for example, and three times more likely to die than an artilleryman. These and others were the army's fighting corps – the army's 'teeth', while all the others were the 'tail' – the service corps who serviced the 'teeth'. 'Tail' corps with average strength included the Royal Army Medical Corps (RAMC, 106,228), the Army Chaplains'

Department (1,999), the Women's Army Auxiliary Corps (26,181), the Nursing Services (14,679), the Army Veterinary Corps (18,655) and the Military Police (6,650). As an infantryman and a 'teeth', Jack Youll was statistically thirty-times more likely to be killed than his 'tail' comrade.[11]

More British soldiers died in the Great War than in the Second World War, which lasted longer and was larger in scale. For details we turn to two monumental books: *Statistics of the Military Effort of the British Empire During the Great War, 1914–1920* published by the War Office in 1922, and *History of the Great War, Based on Official Documents: Medical Services: Casualties and Medical Statistics of the Great War* (1931).[12] Here are some of the revealing facts conveniently and helpfully summarised for us by Tony Ball.[13] All numbers are approximate:

- British, Dominion and Indian forces lost 908,371 dead, mostly British Army: 704,803 (77.6 per cent)
- British, Dominion and Indian forces suffered 1,664,950 wounded, mostly British Army (79.7 per cent)
- Most fatalities occurred on the Western Front: 648,376 (84.8 per cent; the Italian Front sustained 2,090 deaths (0.3 per cent)
- Cause of death:
  Enemy action: 86 per cent
  Sickness and injury: 14 per cent
- Of total casualties there were 2.9 million battle casualties and 5.9 million non-battle casualties – a ratio of 1:2
- The Regiment took 841 officer fatalities, as follows:
  Lieutenant Colonel 14
  Major 17
  Captain 157
  Lieutenant 165
  Second Lieutenant 488
- Medical services treated 1,989,969 wounded men on the Western Front alone; 526,159 further casualties never made it into the medical system

- 80 per cent of those who died, died in the field
- An unusual piece of good news: once in the system you were likely to come out of it alive: 93 per cent did so
- Cause of wounds treated:
    52 per cent artillery or mortar
    35.5 per cent small arms fire
    9.7 per cent the effects of gas
    2 per cent from grenades
    0.3 per cent bayonet wounds
- Location of wounds:
    legs and feet 29.9 per cent
    torso 22 per cent
    arms and hands 21.4 per cent
    head and neck 17.5 per cent
    multiple locations 9.2 per cent
- No trauma statistics are available for the unfortunate men who died
- 64 per cent of the injured returned to front line duty; 18 per cent were declared fit for rear line duties only; 8 per cent were discharged on medical grounds, while 7 per cent died
- Gas wounded: between 93 and 97 per cent returned to duties after 28 days in hospital from 1915; 3.2 per cent of gas wounded died
- In addition to the wounded, the medical services treated 3,528,486 men who were sick and/or injured, with admissions made up largely as follows: venereal disease (VD/STIs), nephritis and dysentery
- Mortality related to the sick and injured was caused in these pre-antibiotic days mostly by: pneumonia, meningitis, nephritis, TB and typhoid
- 84 per cent of sick and injured returned to front line duty, with 9 per cent passed for rear area duties and 4 per cent discharged. 1 per cent died.
- There were 1,245,535 instances of the much-hoped-for 'Blighty Wounds', where a casualty was shipped back to a UK hospital from the Western Front nursing a wound serious enough to warrant

passage but which was unlikely to cause any serious or lasting harm. This represented a huge 62 per cent of the total wounded.
- Of the sick and injured 1,034,160 men were sent back home, 29.3 per cent of the total.
- Significantly, all of the above covers physical trauma; there are no statistics for psychological trauma. Obviously, the reason for this is because conditions such as Post Traumatic Stress Disorder (PTSD) were, in terms of diagnosis and therapy, in their infancy and were yet to be recognised as war wounds under the guise of combat stress, neurasthenia or shell shock. In recent years Dorothy L. Sayers, Pat Barker's *Regeneration Trilogy* and the *Railway Man* (2021) by Eric Lomax have addressed the issues head on, along with clinical research.

Tony Ball focuses on Jack Youll's 11th Battalion in his description of the 'grinding attrition' on individual battalions. On 25 August 1917 an inventory of personnel taken two years after their deployment on the Western Front reveals that of the original thirty-one officers who made the crossing only six had survived (19.35 per cent) and only 243 of the original 985 men survived 24.67 per cent).[14]

Weaponry
What weapons was Jack Youll likely to have had at his disposal for his attacks, holding the line or on patrol?[15] Essentially, the trusty short magazine Lee Enfield rifle No 1 Mark III and the 1907 pattern bayonet. To make the rifle useful he would have 120 rounds of ammunition in his pouches, topped up with one or two bandoliers each containing 50 rounds. Infantry battalions also made use of two heavy machine guns, Maxims or Vickers. By 1918 the latter took over and the gunners were formed into the Machine Gun Corps (average strength 56,987). Additionally, from 1915 336 light, portable Lewis Guns were embedded into infantry platoons. Norman Gladdon was a Lewis gunner.

The hand grenade (usually called 'bomb') had been retired in 1902 due to unreliability and the close range needed for any degree of effectiveness. However, the rifle grenade and the Number 5 Mills Bomb (and later the Number 23) ensured the grenade came back with a resounding and destructive bang.[16]

The mortar likewise missed the start of the war until its re-emergence in 1915 as the trench mortar – a small version of the howitzer. The most effective was the light and portable 3" Stokes.

Training

What level of training would Jack Youll have received on a six months' course?

Musketry (rifles etc)	148 hours per fortnight (24.8 per cent)
Squad Drill	129 (21.5 per cent)
Physical Training	120 (20 per cent)

Field work, Route Marching, Lectures, Bayonet Fighting, Entrenching, Guard and Sentry Duties, Extended Order Drill took up the remaining 33.7 per cent.

Chapter 1

Jack Youll (1897–1918) – His Early Life in Thornley, Co. Durham

What sort of upbringing and early life did Jack Youll have growing up in Thornley? What sort of place was Thornley and how much might it have informed his character and his outlook on life?

Jack was born and grew up in the small mining village of Thornley, the son of Richard William Youll and Margaret Youll, who lived at 'Thorncroft'. This was one of the houses in the terrace known as 'The Villas' and was a substantial property compared with the miners' dwellings in the village.[1] Richard Youll was a pit head weighman and secretary of the Thornley insurance section of The Miners Permanent Relief Fund. From the 1901 Census, taken when Jack was three years old, we see that both parents were 42 and he had four older siblings: Thomas William (19), Ann (12), Jane (10) and Mary (7). There was a young maid, Elizabeth Richardson (16), and it seems that either Richard's or Margaret's father, William, lived with them, at the age of 72 – a good age for a man who could well have been a miner.

Thornley is a former mining village and parish in County Durham, about 5 miles to the east of Durham, 12 miles north-west of Hartlepool, and about 14 miles south-west of Sunderland.

The same census reveals that near relatives Margaret (66) from Gosforth and William Youll (44) lived nearby at the Queen's Head Inn on Hartlepool Street, with Margaret designated as publican and William (Richard's brother, Jack's uncle) a coal miner/stone man. Their two single sons Matthew (24) and Gibson (22) were both hewers in the mine. Matthew was born in nearby Shotton. In 1891 Matthew and then

Gibson had been grocer's apprentices. The maid, Elizabeth J. Welsh, was 14 and hailed from Castle Eden.

Ten years on Jack's sister Mary was still single and described as 'mother's help', presumably replacing the maid who has no entry in the 1911 census at their address. At the Queen's Head, son Matthew (34) had taken over the running of the pub with wife Hannah Mary (28) from Trimdon Grange and 4-year-old Matthew and servant Isabella Close (16) from Brandon Colliery. Jack's older brother, Thomas W. (29 in 1911) was a colliery joiner and lived at 'The Villas' in Thornley with wife Jane Anne (32).

The 1881 Census tells us that another Matthew Youll (age 4) was the son of Joseph (miner) and Margaret Youll of 25 Park Street, Thornley. He had a younger brother (2), confusingly called Gibson.

The 1861 census has Yeuls or Youls living at Dyke Row – William (b. 1829) was a miner; in 1851 we have four male Youls who seem to have come from Newcastle and were all miners.

The mine, and the mining community it fostered, would have had an influence on Jack's early life. The mine made a significant contribution to the Durham Coalfield, producing at its height around 9,000 tons of coal weekly and through its output was a key factor in the growth of Hartlepool and West Hartlepool as a port with the railway link it enjoyed between the two towns.[2] Thornley miners were instrumental in the formation of the Durham Miners' Association, whose inaugural meeting was held in the grounds of the Half-Way House pub in 1869.

Before coal, Thornley was 'a wild and thinly populated area', traversed by pilgrims travelling from the shrine of St Hild, in Hartlepool (c. 614–680), to that of St Cuthbert, in Durham City. Indeed, the bank that the A181 rises over to the west of the village is still known as Signing Hill. Here, pilgrims caught their first glimpse of Durham Cathedral and made the sign of the cross.

Pre-coal, Thornley's population hovered about the fifty mark, mainly farmers. *The Northern Echo* (5 May 2013) describes how coal came to the village and changed it forever:

Jack Youll (1897–1918) – His Early Life in Thornley, Co. Durham

'Then came coal. It was discovered on January 29, 1834, 80ft down in the Five Quarter seam. By the time of the 1841 census, Thornley's population had exploded to 2,730 – all sucked in by the coal to create a wild community living in wild conditions.

'The first to arrive were the shaft-sinkers – specialists from Cornwall and Germany. They were followed by colliery labourers, from Ireland.'

The mine was established in 1835 by John Gully & Partners and was productive until January 1970, when it was closed with the loss of 900 jobs leaving numerous families with little opportunity or prospect for alternative employment.[3] A visit to the village today reveals very little evidence of its industrial and social heritage. Indeed, since the closure of the mine Thornley's fate has been one dictated by the depredations of the wrecking ball: the pub (by then 'The Crossways') has gone, as have the 1843 St Bartholomew's Church, much of the social housing, and the two cinemas, The Hippodrome (1912) and The Ritz (1938).

But the mine and the associated community were thriving when Jack was growing up.[4] He would have worshipped at the church with his family and no doubt frequented the Hippodrome. He attended Thornley Council School before becoming a technical student at a class run by Durham County Council at Wingate. When he was about fifteen he started working for Thornley Colliery in the power station there as an apprentice electrician.

Jane Hatcher describes the development of the village in her *Thornley: A Short History* before and during the years Jack lived there;[5] she tells us that Thornley's population at the 1821 census was only 60, but after the opening of Thornley Colliery in 1835 the new mining settlement began to grow up around it, so that by the 1851 census the population of Thornley had grown to 2,741; the population consisted predominantly of families, rather than single males, for the male/female ratio was 52 per cent to 48 per cent respectively. She adds that:

'A picture of the growing mining village at this time can be obtained from Whellan's *Directory* of 1856,[6] which states that as well as St Bartholomew's Church there was now the Catholic Church of St Godric, which had its own school, and Thornley also had a colliery school, library and newsroom. The colliery was now employing 900 people. Whellan lists 68 directory entries, of which 7 relate to mining, and 15 are pubs!'

Schools in Thornley grew from the early days of the Colliery School which was opposite the colliery and was patronised and partly supported by the Coal Company; 120 or so children were educated in any one school year. When the Board of Education came into being, separate Thornley Boys and Girls Infants departments were opened in 1877. The first Roman Catholic School was built in 1800. There were also Wesleyan and Primitive Methodist Chapels in Thornley from 1871.

In 1865 Thornley supported numerous public-houses; we know their names from a contemporary directory: The Black Bull, The Board Inn, The Engine Tavern, King's Head, The New Inn, Robin Hood, Traveller's Rest, Standish Arms, The Grapes, The Dun Cow and the Three Horse Shoes. Sufficient, surely, to slake the thirst of many a miner. Before that in the main street next to the Market Square and facing the Colliery was the oldest public house, the Colliery Inn. Other public houses included the Station Hotel, built near what was once Thornley's Goods Station; the Railway Tavern, standing near to the weigh cabin on the railway; the Spearman's Arms; and the Queen's Head (Queen Victoria). At the extreme West of the village was the Barrel and Grapes Inn, more commonly known as the Halfway House.

Licensing laws allowed these pubs to open at 6 am and stay open until 11 o'clock in the evening, thus accommodating each of the shifts. Local records tell us that landlords successfully and cynically exploited their patrons by offering sandwiches, pickles and broth to their customers, all liberally sprinkled with thirst-giving salt. The drink fuelled violent sports such as rat coursing, cock fighting and bare knuckle fighting, although there was also pigeon racing, quoits, fives, foot-racing and pot-share bowling for the less antagonistic.

Every village has its characters: Thornley could boast a warm-hearted giant, namely 'Toby Connoly', the village strong man and carrier. He rolled the barrels of beer from the goods station to the various public houses. On one occasion he carried the coffin, single-handed, of a friendless pauper who died in one of the Thornley lodging houses.

Another notable character was 'John the Bum'; he ran plays in the 'Old Gaff'. This was situated near the present site of the Welfare Hall, capable of seating 500–600 people. The orchestra stalls were expensive for those days, namely sixpence, while the pit stalls were fourpence, and the 'gods' or gallery threepence. The entertainments included 'Maria Martin or The Murder in the Red Barn' and other such melodramas. An occasional circus rolled up, while for about six months of every year Barney Berriman's Portable Theatre delighted the villagers with a Shakespearean piece every Wednesday night.

Conditions generally in Thornley were poor to say the least, as they were in all north east mines and mining communities. Wages were miserly, hours long and working conditions hazardous. The poorer miners' houses had bare earth floors just one step down from street level which often led to internal damp. Occupants sat around the fire to maximise the benefit of what warmth there was. Beds consisted of two planks laid on boxes, and were placed in a corner away from the fireplace. Light flickered from candles, water supply had to be brought from a well at Gore Hall Farm by bucket or else bought from the water cart. There were two open air middens where refuse and waste were dumped, although they were rarely emptied.

Direct action to improve matters came with its perils. On 24 November, 1843, warrants were issued for the arrest of sixty-eight Thornley miners, who were absent from the pit without leave. They were on strike and were found guilty at Durham and imprisoned for up to three months.

In an article entitled *The Martyrdom of the Mine – Part One* published 14 June 2019 by the Wheatley Hill History Club,[7] Edward (Neddy)

Rymer describes his first impressions of Thornley in the 1860s. Neddy was a coal miner who worked at pits in Durham, Yorkshire, North Wales, Nottingham and Lancashire. He was a union activist and blacklisted from many coal mines and coalfields as a result of this.

'The first sight of Thornley Colliery made me stare. An awfully black and dismal place it was, with 4,000 people depending on its plant and workings. In one row I counted nine huge heaps of filth lying near and around the pit hovels. Alas! What I saw and heard at Thornley in four years is almost beyond belief.

'There were no visible signs of union at Thornley when I shifted into Quarry Row. The house had one room on the floor, with a loft above, reached by a ladder. The tiles were bare and daylight, rain, wind, sleet or snow came in through the crevices. The room was about 14 feet square and had to serve the purposes of bedroom, kitchen, cook-house, wash-house and coal-house. A large hole broken through the wall in one corner served to cool the place in hot weather. It was with difficulty that the ordinary decencies of life could be observed ... A huge fiery heap ran nearly the length of the village and it is safe to say that half a million tons of coal, broken wood, shale etc. were burning at one time. The smoke and stench from the fiery mountain were often unbearable. In consequence of this state of things socially, drinking, gambling, fighting and reckless pastimes were universal and went unchecked.

'At the office on pay Friday there used to be many hundreds of men who rushed, yelled and forced their way like savages to receive their wages ... I made the acquaintance of many of the best people at Thornley, including Bill Norman, one of the leaders in the strike of 1844 and William Beaney, the noted school-master and Primitive Methodist local preacher. From both of these men I received many valuable lessons and much advice. Norman put me in the way of writing the first letter I ever sent to the Press and recommended me to a few good books which I needed in my struggle.'

By the end of century the standard of living improved. Women and children were prohibited from work in the mine, the length of the shift was shortened and wages increased.[8] The Durham Miners' Association was established and the miners were more secure in the knowledge that they had a Union which would safeguard their rights and fight to improve their social and working conditions.

Founded in 1869, the union membership soon rose to 4,000, but within a year had receded to 2,000; nevertheless in December 1870, William Crawford became the union's president, and rebuilt its membership to become the largest miners' union in the UK.

In 1881 the population stood at 3,132, while in 1891 it had fallen to 2,070 when many left the village after the pit owner's bankruptcy and an extended pause in the payment of wages.

According to Sidney Webb (1859–1947), socialist, economist, social reformer, co-founder of the London School of Economics and early member of the Fabian Society, action in 1890 ensured that the district was the first in the country to adopt a standard seven-hour day, while the long strike of 1892 against a proposed 15 per cent cut in wages was resolved with an agreement to accept a 10 per cent cut. By 1900, membership had risen to 80,000.

While the DMA represented most miners in County Durham, some in specialist jobs were represented by the Durham County Colliery Enginemen's Association, the Durham Colliery Mechanics' Association, and the Durham Cokemen's Association.

Such was the employment situation in which Jack Youll found himself when he left school to become an apprentice electrician at the colliery.

A state of war existed between Great Britain from 11.00 pm on 4 August 1914 and the First World War intruded on life in Thornley, while many men duly joined up: some paid the ultimate sacrifice, as could be seen in the War Memorial erected in the first Miners' Welfare Hall. John Scott Youll was, of course, one of these men, the brother of one of the founder members of the Thornley Workers' Institute. When in 1944 the Miners' Welfare Hall was destroyed by fire that War Memorial went up with it.[9]

The Naval Reserve was mobilised followed by the Army Reserve and the Territorial Force. It did not take long before a Thornley man was killed in action. On 22 September Stoker Francis Veitch, age 17, of Hartlepool Street died when a German submarine (*U9*) sank three RN armoured cruisers – HMS *Aboukir*, HMS *Hogue* and HMS *Cressy* in the Atlantic. Veitch was on the *Hogue* which took two torpedoes; 837 men were rescued but 1,459 men died, mainly cadets and reservists.[10] Willliam Barratt, brother-in-law of James Burley, manager of the Palace Theatre in Wheatley Hill, was reported missing when HMS *Aboukir* went down. He was 35-years-old and father to two children.

The Veitch family of Hartlepool Street suffered a further tragic misfortune in December 1916 when their son-in-law, Drummer Stanley Wright of the East Yorks, died from wounds received in action on 27 November. The drummer was one of the first Thornley men to sign up. Their daughter, of 'The Villas', Thornley, was left widowed and their two children fatherless, the younger of whom Drummer Wright never saw.

So the men of Thornley responded with gusto to the call for arms to be taken up 'to curb the excessive tyranny of the German Emperor' so that when a recruiting officer visited the area he would depart with a haul of over 150 recruits. At the same time the local authorities were mindful of the social and domestic ramifications of this exodus of young men:

> 'The task of looking after the wives and families of reservists who have been called up has already been commenced by Miss Curry of Thornley House and Dr J. Ryan of the Knoll, Wheatley Hill, who have undertaken the duties of local secretaries of Queen Mary's Fund … it was decided to seek information relating to the application of the Durham County relief fund to cases of distress among civilians … the Chairman pointed out that the wives and children of soldiers were being provided for.'

The residents of Thornley 'resolved to protest to the Board of Trade against the excessive prices of foodstuffs, especially flour and ask that remedial steps be taken on behalf of the poor and working classes' in these straitened times.[11]

The war too naturally had an impact on the Miner's Council whose membership was 'either being laid idle altogether or who are working very slack time'. Payment of the full allowance would have 'crippled' the Council, so the Executive Committee ruled that 'men out of work be paid 10s a week' and contributions were increased accordingly.

Thornley War Relief fund was to extend the benefits of their fatal accident fund to cases of men being killed in the war or of dying from disease while on active service. Miss Hill, meanwhile, reported that members of the sewing guild had collected £16.6s.1d.[12]

Thornley residents were helping the Belgian Relief Fund with a meeting at the Hippodrome which raised £16.6s.7d and a Saturday night dance at the Roman Catholic School.

By spring 1915 reports of casualties, soldiers missing and wounded and local men taken prisoner of war were arriving thick and fast, as was the news of the debilitating and lethal effects of poisonous gas.[13]

Meanwhile, aspects of life in Thornley and, in particular, Youll family life, went on. In September 1915:

> 'Thornley Parish Church was the venue for the wedding of Miss Annie Youll, eldest daughter of Mr William and Mrs Richard Youll of 'The Villas', Thornley, and Mr Richard Heckels Tully, of Newcastle. The bride, who wore a pretty lime-coloured costume, was attended by her youngest sister, Miss Mary Youll, as bridesmaid. She was given away by her father. Mr James A. Tully, brother of the bridegroom, was best man.'[14]

To give a vivid picture of Jack Youll's Thornley and life there at the outbreak of war, as well as what was going on at the front, here are a number of extracts from *The Employees and Residents of Thornley*:

'The women of Thornley and Wheatley Hill (virtually contiguous) came together in October 1914 and succeeded in making and sending the following wonderful fruits of their labours to the front:

> 307 shirts
> 145 pairs of socks
> 57 handkerchiefs
> 19 pairs of blankets
> 3 pairs of pillow cases
> 2 helmets
> 3 dozen tins of Vaseline
> bandages

along with some whiffs, cigarettes and tobacco. Shirts and socks were laundried and the socks were liberally doused in boric acid before they were sent off.'

It was not unusual for a family to send more than one member to the front:

'There is the Lawson family, of which four brothers are in the army and one in the navy. A son-in-law, Edward McDermott, is a private in the Durham Light Infantry. These five patriotic sons ... are George, a driver in the Royal Army Service Corps; Thomas, a private in the Tyneside Irish; Fred, a gunner in the RFA; Harry, a stoker in the Royal Navy; and Jacob, the youngest, a driver in the Royal Army Service Corps.'

Mrs Cook, a widow of Thornley, had two sons in the navy and two in the army:

'Michael is on the Battleship *Russell*. And was present when the vessel shelled with deadly accuracy, at five miles range, the German submarine factory at Zeebrugge. George is on the light cruiser *Sapphire*. The last letter his mother received from him was from the

'Gulf of Somewhere' [censored]. The two army boys are Stanley, in the Tyneside Commercials, and Malcolm in the Royal Army Service Corps.'

By January 1915, Mr and Mrs Joseph Hutchinson of Thornley could claim five sons – all in the Northumberland Fusiliers: Privates William, Thomas, Joseph, Christopher and Thompson.

Mr and Mrs Thompson from Ludworth had six sons in the army, all in different regiments:

'Driver A. Thompson, Northumberland RFA; Lance Corporal M. Thompson, 10th DLI; Pte Jack Thompson, 1st Leicester Regiment; Pte James Thompson, Yorkshire Regiment; Pte Alf Thompson, 11th DLI and Pte Charles Thompson, West Yorks Regiment.'

Private Robert Griffiths of the DLI (Territorials) regales his wife back in Thornley with a description of his new accommodation:

'I live in a house on my own here; it is rent free and free of rates. It is a hole dug in the ground about three feet deep. There are a lot of tree branches over the top and then clay and 'muck' on top of the branches. It is a very nice house, and is nicely situated, and very sloppy when it rains. Instead of going upstairs to bed, we go downstairs. We see some terrible queer sights out here.'

Sapper William Wick, a miner from Thornley, finds it surprising:

'How many public houses there are in this country. Almost every house sells beer, and the people are living close to the firing line. The town I am speaking of is shelled every day ... to see women and children running about here you would not think there was a war going on.'

In May 1915 we get another reference to the toxic and deadly effects of German gas: Private Richard Gaskell from Thornley was hospitalised in Rouen suffering from the effects of gas:

> 'This awful gas the Germans are using to beat us. I can tell you it's terrible, nothing but brutal murder … it has left me with pains in my chest and sides and sometimes I have a numb feeling and dizziness … when we had to retire from the trenches to get away from the gas we had to cross the open fields. The Germans were ready for us. For they turned on their Maxim guns, rifles. 'Jack Johnsons'. Dirty big black boxes, shrapnel and bursting shells of gas. I am sure they sent thousands over in two hours. It was like hell upon earth.'

Jack Johnson was a famous American boxer who became the first African-American world heavyweight boxing champion (1908–1915). Johnson was front page news all over the world for his skills in the boxing ring and for the incidents in his private life that came with fame, money and tensions around race in the US at that time. The sporting pages of newspapers, read avidly by soldiers on the Front, were filled with tales of Jack Johnson whose name was on everyone's lips. British troops in the trenches borrowed his famous name to describe the powerful black-coloured German 150mm heavy artillery shells that exploded with devastating force and plumes of black smoke.[15] 'Black Maria' and 'coal box' were synonyms.

The miners' strike back in England was not received well, at least by Private Daniel Connor of the 2nd Durhams:

> 'It is awful to think that men could be so callous as to go on strike at a time when they are endangering their brothers lives out here as well as their own. They are surely killing men out here as are the German guns … they don't know what their conduct at home means to the men out here.'

Jack Youll (1897–1918) – His Early Life in Thornley, Co. Durham

Sapper George Oswald, one of four Thornley men who went out to France to do mining work, describes his experiences to Mr John Rivers, under-manager of Thornley Colliery:

> 'We blew a mine up ... you should have seen the Germans go up in the air. We could hear them working underneath us.'

Mr Rivers also received a very descriptive letter from Private Edward Kears of the 10th DLI:

> 'We lost half a battalion; I thought every moment was my last ... I cannot describe what it was like, and I don't want to go through another one like it. There was kit flying all over the place. I lost everything I had. Not far away from me a poor chap had his head taken clean off. They were shouting for stretcher bearers all night.'

On 10 December 1915, the Thornley War Relief Committee and the Women's Guild organised a parcel for each soldier and sailor on active service who lived or worked at Thornley Colliery. Each parcel contained:

¼ lb of plug tobacco
¼ lb of tobacco mixture
100 cigarettes
a pipe
chocolates or peppermint and other acceptable little items

All together 212 parcels were sent out at a cost of £68.00.

With winter in full swing, frostbite added to the manifold problems of trench life, as this letter of 10 December from Private 'Bob' Lofthouse, from Shadforth Terrace, Ludworth makes clear:

> 'Winter is with us, and up to the present it is similar to our English weather: rain, mud, snow and ice and cold dull days. We have to be

extra careful to keep free from frostbite. Our feet are greased during frosts in the trenches, and we rub them on every opportunity. We all have goatskin coats and long waterproof coats … Long boots are given to us before we go into the trenches, and we need them. In some places the water is above the knees. It's champion when you stick in the mud and pull your legs out of the boots … when we get to our dugout we change our socks, and all's well …all food is brought up at night … bread, biscuits, bacon, jam, boiled beef and cheese … plenty of sand and soil drops into the food.'

Early in the New Year, 14 January 1916, Bob informs us again, this time with his obvious penchant for ornithology – a rare glimpse of wildlife in this cauldron of destruction:

'Many birds have passed to and fro across the firing line these last few weeks. Meadow pipits, larks, tits and wood pigeons. I saw a flock of the latter; there were about sixty … sometimes the goldfinch passes, also the brown linnet … sometimes the chaffinch gives us a call … a few hawks have been passing these last few days … mostly sparrow hawks and a few kestrels. A beautiful large falcon haunted our lines for two days about the middle of December. The day after Christmas Day was fine and mild, and I heard a thrush singing.'

Bob goes on to spot blackbirds, magpies, rooks and starlings, and mallard. One day four herons passed, he heard the golden plover at night. In February 1916 Private Charles Bainbridge wrote to George Barker of Dalton House, Thornley in between his posting from Gallipoli to Salonika and a totally different form of wildlife – 'dirt with legs on':

'When we do get warm we know about it. Why do we know it? Well, I have a division living on me now … I am covered in dirt with legs on, and why do I say division? Well, because they are like soldiers – as soon as you kill one another takes its place. At night before getting into 'kip' we have a proper scratch around ourselves ... then they start galloping up and down our backs like racehorses.'

For another change of scenery we get a letter from Gunner Benjamin Robinson who is serving in the same battery as his father in Egypt and writes to his aunt from Egypt:

'We are not allowed to go into the Arabian Quarter, because two of our men were knocked out by the natives. The houses are a disgrace. The people live with pigs, hens, goats and horses and the streets are very narrow. The general condition of things reminds one of the Plague of London.'

The Daily Jeopardy in a Miner's Life

When Jack Youll reached the sodden and hazardous trenches of the Western Front, he may have derived some small benefit from the fact that he had experienced life in a community that was inured to danger, hard graft, death, serious injury and serial bereavement. Any miner who served in either of the World Wars will tell you that while there are significant differences, there are many similarities, not least with the troops involved in tunnelling under the German lines.

If there is any doubt as to the danger involved in mining, here is a list of those killed at work in Thornley – and these are just the 'A's:

Adamson, Frederick, 27 May 1914, aged 21, Wagon Runner, deceased was found between the last buffer of a set of 10 wagons which he had braked down and secured, and the first buffer of a set of 10 wagons, none of the brakes of which were down; it is not known how he got there

Anderson, Herbert, 8 Jan 1931, (*accident*: 3 Jan 1931), aged 22, Putter, kicked by pony

Archbold, William, 19 Nov 1860, aged 12, Mason, killed by a fall of stone

Archer, W., 25 Jun 1940, aged 43, Sawer (Temp.), caught by saw

Armstrong, G., 7 Feb 1867, aged 12, Door Keeper, killed by a set of tubs in engine plane while getting off; riding contrary to orders

Armstrong, John, 5 Aug 1841, aged 15, Putter, killed in the 1841 explosion, *Buried*: St. Helen's Parish Church/Cemetery, Kelloe

Armstrong, Robert, 29 Sep 1864, aged 14, Pony Putter, killed by a fall of stone

Arnold, James, 17 Dec 1912, aged 16, Driver, with other drivers he was standing at the inbye end of the landing waiting for the empty set; a set of full tubs was standing ready to go out; when the empty set came in it was derailed at the points by some loose stone and fouled the standing full set pushing it down the handing; the main rope between the ways, set swinging by the derailment, knocked the lad under the full tubs as they were pushed back; when an empty set is entering a landing in which a full set is standing, it is highly desirable that persons and horses should be kept at a safe distance from the inbye end of the full set, *Buried*: Wheatley Hill Cemetery

Atchinson, Thomas Henry, 20 Dec 1943, aged 16, Landing Lad, death from asphyxia caused through being caught under a tub of coal

Atkinson, George, 17 Oct 1940, aged 64, Overman, killed by a fall of stone

Avery, William, 1 Oct 1855, aged 14, Lamp Keeper, crushed by the cage

Of the eleven fatalities seven were mere boys: two were 12, two were 14, one was 15 and two were 16.

Source: Durham Mining Museum
http://www.dmm.org.uk/colliery/t002.htm

We also know that on 5 August 1841, an explosion in the Harvey seam killed nine workers. One was 42-year-old Thomas Haswell, who left a wife and seven children. The other eight victims were boys aged between 9 and 17. The following year, the Mines and Collieries Act prohibited children from working more than ten hours a day underground.

Chapter 2

Jack Youll and the 1st Durham Engineers

About one year after the start of the First World War Jack clearly decided that he needed to answer the call and to put his training as an electrician to some patriotic use – it may, of course, be that his apprenticeship had come to an end and, being now of military age, he simply took this as his first opportunity to sign up. Whatever, he enlisted at Jarrow on 1 July 1916 at the age of 18, and joined the Royal Engineers by way of the 1/1st Durham Field Company or 1st Durham Engineers, a territorial unit.

The 1st Durham Engineers, who in 1910 had been redesignated as the Durham Fortress Engineers, with the addition of the Electric Light Company provided by the Tyne Electrical Engineers (formerly Submarine Miners), was a volunteer unit of the Royal Engineers.[1] First founded in 1868 it occasionally operated with the Tyne Electrical Engineers, while at other times it acted as an independent unit. Its primary sphere of operation was defence of the north-east coast of England, but it also sent detachments on active service to the Suakin Expedition,[2] the Second Boer War (1899–1902),[3] and Italy during the First World War.

The Fortress Engineers had facilities in Jarrow and Gateshead with the HQ at Western Road in Jarrow, and formed part of North Eastern Coastal Defences.

We learn from Major O.M. Short that:[4]

'When the TF was mobilised on the outbreak of war in August 1914, the Durham Fortress Engineers took up their places in the North Eastern Coastal Defences. At first they were employed on constructing field defences, erecting hutted camps, etc. By the summer of 1915 there were three strong lines of entrenchments, bomb-proof shelters and dug-outs linking strongpoints and gun positions along the coast as well as the fixed defences at Tynemouth and Hartlepool.'

Presumably some of this activity was triggered by the German navy's bombardment of nearby Hartlepool and West Hartlepool on 16 December 1914 – a hugely significant event in the early war which Jack Youll missed but which he would have heard plenty about.[5] The intense patriotism and the desire for revenge the attack generated – along with the bombardments further down the coast at Whitby and Scarborough – would surely still be felt by the time Jack Youll joined up. Who knows, it may have been a factor in Jack's decision to enlist in the first place.

Despite the bombardments, and Zeppelin raids in January and June 1915, it became increasingly clear that Germany was not going to invade Britain so it was an easy decision to deploy these engineers on active service overseas as Field Companies where the need was substantial.[6]

This is how these Field Companies were constituted and deployed:

1st Durham Field Company
1st Durham Field Company joined 4th Division in France on 20 September 1915 and served with it on the Western Front to the end of the war. It was renumbered 526th (Durham) Field Company, RE, in February 1917.

2nd Durham Field Company
2nd Durham Field Company joined 5th Division in France, also on 20 September 1915, and served with it on the Western Front until November 1917, when the division was transferred to the Italian Front. 5th Division returned to the Western Front in April 1918 and fought there until the end of the war. It was renumbered 527th (Durham) Field Company, RE, in February 1917.

3rd Durham Field Company

3rd Durham Field Company landed at Le Havre on 18 September 1915 and joined 51st (Highland) Division on 19 September, towards the end of the Battle of the Somme. On 30 January 1916 it transferred to 7th Division (in exchange for a Highland Field Company) and served with it on the Western Front until November 1917, when the division was transferred to the Italian front. 7th Division then served in Italy until the end of the war. It was renumbered 528th (Durham) Field Company, RE, in February 1917.

And so Jack Youll found himself in France in August 1916 as a Royal Engineer.

Chapter 3

A Very Short History of The Northumberland Fusiliers 1674–1918

Often known as the 'Fighting Fifth' because the regiment was called the Fifth Foot until 1881, the Northumberland Fusiliers raised no fewer than fifty-one battalions for service in the First World War, thus making it the second largest after the London Regiment.

Having trained for a year or so with the Durham Engineers, Jack was posted to France on 11 August and it soon became clear that his obvious talents marked him out as officer material. The result was that he was recommended for officer training, and returned to England on 22 February 1917 to begin his course. That June it was announced that he would be gazetted as a temporary second lieutenant in the 1st Northumberland Fusiliers (later the Royal Northumberland Fusiliers), before returning to the Western Front a month later attached to the regiment's 11th Battalion as a temporary second lieutenant.

In 1674, King Charles II (r. 1660–1685) signed the Treaty of Westminster bringing to an end three years of conflict with the Dutch Republic. Part of the settlement required four auxiliary regiments to be raised and attached to the Dutch army to help them in their fight against the French. One of these auxiliaries was formed in Ireland under Daniel O'Brien, Viscount Clare. The Royal Northumberland Fusiliers was one of three 'English' units in the Dutch Anglo-Scots Brigade, a brigade of British soldiers of fortune, which usually comprised six infantry regiments, three recruited primarily from Scotland and three from England.

In 1685, the regiment returned briefly to England to help Charles's brother and successor, James II, put down what we now know as the Monmouth Rebellion (or the Pitchfork Rebellion) – an attempt to depose James II when a group of dissident Protestants led by James Scott, 1st Duke of Monmouth, eldest illegitimate son of Charles II, opposed James largely on account of the fact that he was a Catholic . Three years later, the regiment came with William of Orange, leader of the Dutch Republic, when he invaded England. The 'Glorious Revolution' led to William replacing James on the throne.

A consequence of this was that the regiment was now formally part of the British Army, and as such continued to fight for William during the Nine Years War (1688–97), a conflict between the nations of the Grand Alliance and France, serving first in Ireland, fighting at the Battle of the Boyne (1690) as well as participating in the sieges of Athlone and Limerick (1691). In 1692 it left for Flanders, before returning to Ireland in 1698.

The regiment then fought in Spain from 1707 to 1712 in the War of the Spanish Succession (1702–13) before moving to Gibraltar – captured in 1704 by the Anglo-Dutch fleet of the Grand Alliance – for sixteen years of garrison service. That day saw from dawn and for the next five hours, some 15,000 cannon fired from the fleet into the city. In 1751 it took the official name of the 5th Regiment of Foot, reflecting its ranking in the infantry. During the Seven Years' War (1756–63) it participated in raids on the French coast and saw action in Germany at Warburg (1760) and Wilhelmsthal (1762).

In 1768, Hugh Percy, the eldest son of the Duke of Northumberland, was made colonel of the 5th Foot and remained in post for sixteen years, leading it through the American War of Independence (1775–83).

The regiment was shipped to Boston, Massachusetts in May 1774 and so was in situ when the fighting started, engaging in a series of battles, including Lexington and Bunker Hill (both 1775), Long Island (1776) and Brandywine Creek (1777).

1778 saw it transfer to St Lucia in the West Indies and able to add a white hackle to its uniform to mark a famous victory over a much superior French force on St Lucia that same year.[1] The French lost 400 killed and 1,100 wounded to the British losses of 10 killed and 130 wounded, which included two officers from the 5th Foot. After two years the regiment sailed to Ireland in December 1780.

It was in 1782 that the regiment gained its official association with Northumberland, becoming the 5th (Northumberland) Regiment of Foot, the county being chosen as a compliment to the colonel, Hugh Percy, 1st Duke of Northumberland.

The next posting was to Canada in 1787 where it remained for ten years, before returning to Britain. In 1799, it formed a 2nd Battalion, which lasted until 1816.

During the early years of the Peninsular War (1808–14), 1st Battalion fought in Portugal at Roliça and Vimeiro (both 1808), and Corunna (1809), before joining the Walcheren expedition in the Netherlands. It was in Portugal that it earned the nicknames the 'Old and Bold', 'The Fighting Fifth' and also 'Lord Wellington's Bodyguard'. It formed part of a small force which beat off an overwhelming body of the enemy at El Boden in 1811, a performance which Wellington notified to the Army as 'a memorable example of what can be done by steadiness, discipline, and confidence'.

It was replaced by 2nd Battalion, which served at Bussaco (1810), Fuentes d'Onoro and Ciudad Rodrigo (1812). Both battalions were then in action at Salamanca (also 1812).

We learn from Major Ridge[2] that Wellington, at the siege of Ciudad Rodrigo in early January 1812, struck lucky when 'the magnificent 5th Foot', in the words of Allan Mallinson:

> 'Managed to get a lodgement atop the wall; and how they did so says much about the army's fighting spirit then and since. For the first man into the fortress that night was not a thrusting ensign fresh from the playing fields of Eton, nor a hardened serjeant (sic) who knew how to fight, nor a corporal keen for his extra stripe, nor even one of Wellington's 'scum of the earth', a rum-fuelled private soldier from the coal hovels of the Tyne or wherever the 5th managed to find their men.[3] It was in fact their Commanding Officer, Lieutenant

Colonel Henry Ridge. To protect himself against the missiles raining down from the battlements, he told a handful of his men to hold their muskets above his head in an umbrella of bayonets, and to advance up the ladder behind him. When they reached the end of the ladder, a good 15 feet short of the top of the wall, he told one of them to stand on the top rung, and another to climb on to his shoulders, and then he, Ridge, climbed on to the second man's shoulders, and hauled himself over the parapet. He was cut down and killed soon afterwards, but not before his men were swarming over the battlements.'[4]

1st Battalion went on to serve at Vitoria and Nivelle (both 1813), and Orthez and Toulouse (1814), as well as moving to Canada for the War of 1812 (1812–15). In 1815, it was back in Europe for the Waterloo campaign, fighting alongside 2nd Battalion again at the storming of Cambrai.

On 23 April 1836 it was designated a fusilier unit, becoming the 5th Regiment of Foot (Northumberland Fusiliers). From then on, it sported a badge featuring a flaming grenade. It was also allowed to incorporate its 'ancient badge', an image of St George slaying a dragon.

After the Napoleonic Wars, the regiment was stationed in the West Indies, the Mediterranean, Ireland and Mauritius. In 1857, it raised a second 2nd Battalion which remained at home, while 1st Battalion was sent to serve in the Indian Mutiny (1857–88).

1st Battalion returned to India in 1866, staying for fourteen years and forming part of the Peshawar Field Force during the Second Afghan War (1878–80). It was replaced in India by 2nd Battalion in 1880. The latter took part in the Black Mountain Expedition on the North-West Frontier in 1888.

As a result of the 1881 Childers Reforms which reorganised the infantry regiments of the British Army, the regiment's name changed yet again, now becoming The Northumberland Fusiliers.

In 1895 1st Battalion sent a detachment to the Gold Coast (Ghana) in West Africa for the Fourth Ashanti War. The entire battalion then fought in the Sudan in 1898 and on the North-West Frontier of India in 1908.

Both regular battalions then participated in the Second Boer War (1899–1902), engaging in several battles, including Belmont, Graspan, Modder River, Magersfontein, Stormberg, Reddersberg and Sanna's Post.

Such were the demands of this war that the regiment raised two additional regular battalions in 1900. 3rd Battalion served in South Africa, while 4th Battalion was stationed in Ireland – both were disbanded in 1907.[5]

The Northumberland Fusiliers and the First World War

We have already seen how the First World War started and the main players in that global conflict. We can now start to examine the role of Jack Youll in the war with a look at his regiment, at the 1st Battalion which he initially signed up with, and at the 11th Battalion in which he served in France and Italy. He was mentioned in despatches at Polygon Wood, while Asiago in Italy was where he won his Victoria Cross and Italian Silver Star. Italy was also the place where he was killed in action during the Battle of Vittorio Veneto.

The National Army Museum tells us that:

'The Northumberland Fusiliers raised 50 Reserve, Territorial, New Army, Garrison and Home Service battalions for the First World War (1914–18), a number only bettered by the 88 battalions of the all-territorial London Regiment. 29 of the Northumberland battalions served overseas, earning 67 battle honours in France and Flanders, Salonika, Gallipoli, Egypt and Italy.[6]

'Of its regular units, 1st Battalion spent the whole of the conflict on the Western Front, arriving there in August 1914 and going on to fight in many of the main engagements. 2nd Battalion was in India on the outbreak of war, but deployed to France in January 1915. Later that year, it was transferred to Egypt and then to Salonika.'[7]

The regiment suffered over 16,000 killed in action with thousands more wounded to varying extents. The 1st Battalion incurred 1,786 KIAs, the 2nd 1,724. The 11th Battalion lost 498 men from 26 August 1915 in France, Flanders and Italy. Psychological impairment would have been higher still, with countless cases of PTSD. It won five Victoria Crosses.[8]

The regiment was predominantly engaged in trench warfare on the Western Front in Belgium and France, but also participated in fighting on the Macedonian front, the Gallipoli Campaign, the Sinai and Palestine Campaign and the Italian Front.

On the outbreak of the war, the Northumberland Fusiliers were made up of seven battalions:

- The 1st and 2nd Battalions of the Regular Army, in common with all line infantry regiments of the British Army at this time, were deployed as one at home (1st Battalion at Portsmouth) and the other overseas (2nd Battalion at Sabathu, India)
- The 3rd (Reserve) Battalion of the Special Reserve (SR) – the former Northumberland Light Infantry Regiment of Militia – was transferred to the Special Reserve by Haldane's military reforms in 1908
- The 4th, 5th, 6th, and 7th Battalions of the Territorial Force formed the Territorial Force's Northumberland Brigade of the Northumbrian Division.
  According to https://www.britishempire.co.uk/forces/ armyunits/britishinfantry/northumberland.htm#

The 1st Battalion

The 1st was part of the 9th Brigade, commanded by Brigadier General Shaw, in General Haldane's 3rd Division and it needed 621 reservists to bring it up to war strength. It arrived in France on 14 August 1914 and was soon in action at Mons, in which battle 3rd and 5th Divisions bore the brunt of the fighting, and thereafter saw action in all the major engagements of 1914 – Marne, Aisne, La Bassee, Armentières and Ypres. The battalion remained on the Western Front, in the same brigade and division, for the rest of the war. In all it suffered 1,742 dead.

The 2nd Battalion

The 2nd Battalion arrived home from India in December 1914 and was allocated to the 84th Brigade of the newly formed 28th Division, made up of regular battalions returning from overseas. The battalion arrived in France in January 1915 and its first major action was during the German gas attack at Second Ypres and in the ensuing battles. It was then in the trenches at Kemmel and in the fighting in the Hohenzollern Redoubt. In November 1915 the 28th Division was sent to Macedonia, where malaria took a greater toll than the enemy. On one occasion a company paraded with just one officer and two lance-corporals: malaria had accounted for the rest. The battalion remained there till June 1918, when it returned to France and joined 150th Brigade in the reconstituted 50th (Northumbrian) Division, a Territorial division; it stayed with that division to the end of the war. Total dead 709 of which 392 were battle casualties.

So, the 1st Battalion was sent to Portsmouth on 4 August 1914, as part of 9th Brigade, 3rd Division. Landing at Havre on 14 August. On 11 November 1918 when the armistice was signed they were located at La Longueville, east of Bavai, France.

Chapter 4

11th Northumberland Fusiliers in France

The 11th (Service) Battalion, an element of the 23rd Division and part of 68 Brigade, to which Jack Youll was attached as a temporary second lieutenant was formed at Newcastle in September 1914 as part of Kitchener's Third New Army, moving to Bullswater, near Frensham, Guildford as part of 68th Brigade, 23rd Division; they were accompanied by 69th and 70th Brigades. Chris Baker tells us that 'the infantry battalions raised as part of the New Armies were known as Service Battalions, simply to distinguish them as having been raised for war service only and not as a permanent addition to the Armed Forces of the Crown. In every other respect they were organised and (eventually) equipped in the same way as a regular battalion'.[1]

In December 1914 the battalion moved to North Camp, Aldershot with CII and CIII Artillery Brigades relocating to Ewshott near Farnham. In February 1915 they were at Shorncliffe in Kent with infantry units building defences to the south of London during April and May. Then the Division relocated to Bordon, Hampshire in the Woolmer Forest near Alton.

The third week of August was huge for the Battalion, for it was then that the Division set sail for Boulogne, mustering near Tilques. On 5 September, 23rd Division were attached to III Corps and proceeded to Merris-Vieux Berquin for 'trench familiarisation' under the auspices of 20th (Light) and 27th Divisions. On 14 September the Division assumed responsibility for the front line between Ferme Grande Flamengrie and the Armentières-Wez-Macquart road.

The Battle of Loos (25 September to 8 October 1915) saw the Division hold the front at Bois Grenier, from which they were relieved at the end of January 1916 while Divisional HQ was established at Blaringhem and the troops were given a period of rest around Bruay. This lasted to 3 March when they returned to the front line and took over a sector between Boyeau de l'Ersatz and the Souchez river from the French 17th Division, while the artillery assumed an exposed position between Carency and Bois de Bouvigny, themselves attracting heavy shelling.

Early March saw the establishment of a Tunnelling Company: men with a background in mining were transferred from the ranks to the Royal Engineers.

Here is the account of the battles around St Eloi as given by https://www.britishempire.co.uk/forces/armyunits/britishinfantry/northumberland.htm:

'St Eloi, 27 March 1916
'The Germans had built a strong defensive position at the village of St Eloi three miles south of Ypres. The trench had a parapet nine feet high from which machine guns covered the approach and the ground in front was thickly covered with barbed wire entanglements. The British sappers tunnelled up to this position and laid a large store of high explosives below it. At 4.30am on 27 March 1916 they blew it up causing a massive explosion. The Northumberland and Royal Fusiliers were ordered to charge the position as soon as the mine had been detonated. This they did but when they reached the German wire they found that it had not been damaged enough to get through.

'They clambered over and under the wire as best they could and had also to scale the high parapets which were also intact. At the apex of the salient there was a machine-gun crew which fired on the Fusiliers, although this was stopped by the brave action of a subaltern and three men who disabled it with a grenade and bayonet attack. The trench system had been destroyed and a company of Jaegers from Schleswig-Holstein wiped out, but a German counter-attack soon took place. The Fusiliers had come across a large store of grenades which they used against the Germans and repulsed their attack.

'Having got so far and taken many prisoners the two battalions forged on to the second line of enemy trenches, using the large quantity of German grenades they had found. Behind the trenches was a marshy area into which the retreating Germans fled leaving a salient deep inside the enemy lines under British control. For the next few days the German artillery bombarded the position heavily and the Fusiliers were replaced by a Canadian Brigade. The area was the scene of determined attacks and counter-attacks for the next few weeks.'

More R&R came in mid-April at Bruay, lasting until mid-May when they took over the Souchez-Angres front again, just prior to the German attack on Vimy Ridge on 21 May. On 11 June the 23rd Division infantry moved to Bomy and the artillery to Chamblain Chatelain and Therouanne for intensive training for the Battles of the Somme. They saw action at the Battle of Albert, including the capture of Contalmaison, the Battles of Bazentin Ridge, Pozieres, Flers-Courcelette, Morval, and the Battle of Transloy taking part in the capture of Le Sars.

In 1917 there were yet more battles, including those at Messines, Menin Road, Polygon Wood and the First and Second Battles of Passchendaele. In November 1917 the Division would be transferred to Italy and were focussed between Mantua and Marcaria, before taking over the front line at the Montello Hill near Bergamo on 4 December.

Around the time of their move to Italy, Padre S. Hinchliffe of the 26th Battalion, Northumberland Fusiliers gives a graphic and worrying description of life in the sodden, mud sucking trenches:

'Four men had made a gallant attempt to bring up rations. All four lay dead, one with his head blown off. Legs and arms jutted out from shell holes …a rifle shot rang out in front of us, and the word went around that a man had shot his finger off. I didn't believe it. I didn't want to believe that one of my men would have done such a thing.'

1918 brought fighting on the Asiago Plain and the Battle of Vittorio Veneto, and the Battle of the Piave River; dates of considerable significance for Jack Youll. The Italian Armistice took place at 3 pm on 4 November when the 23rd were half way between the rivers Livenza and Meduna, east of Sacile. They moved to billets west of Treviso and were demobbed in January and February 1919.

Chapter 5

11th Northumberland Fusiliers Regimental War Diaries and Orders

From 1907 units in active service were obliged to keep a daily record of events by the Field Service Regulations Part II. These records are War Diaries or Intelligence Summaries. War Diaries were an official document of record and, in theory at least, had to be completed on a daily basis as required by the War Office; each month they were all sent to Brigade HQ whence they were submitted for scrutiny by a higher being. If completed fully and accurately they were extremely valuable and significant because they captured ongoing action in the field, be it front line combat, raids or patrols, or training while in reserve. They documented the reality of the battalions' activity rather than verbiage emanating at HQ level. Much was learned from the proper observance and analysis of the diaries, and tactics and strategy, policy and protocols were modified from the information they conveyed to decision makers.

According to the greatwar.co.uk website:

'The purpose of the War Diary was to create a record of the operations of the unit on active service. It would record the part it was playing in a battle and would usually list the number of men who went into action and the number of casualties when the unit came out of the action. The information in a War Diary would be used by senior commanders for intelligence about the enemy opposite their units and as a historical record for future planning ... The information contained in the daily report of a War Diary can vary from just a few words to a detailed description of life at the Front. It may include map references, individuals' names (usually officers only), awards of gallantry medals and casualty reports. The information contained in the War Diary will reflect the type of unit, for example ... An infantry battalion on the Front Line will record the part it played in a particular battle action or raid. It will also outline the duties carried out during its daily routine out of the line, for example, training, parades, cleaning of equipment and bathing the men, sorting out stores and so on.'

The fact that the War Diary was sometimes written under very difficult conditions when the unit was in action explains why some daily reports were scribbled and brief. Another interesting fact about the War Diaries is that the reports are often a reflection of the individual who was writing them. Some are descriptive, full of detail, map references, names and are also in clear handwriting. Others are matter-of-fact with few details or may have handwriting that is hard to read.[1]

Regimental diaries and Orders can, therefore, be of enormous help in tracking the actions of regiments and battalions in the field. Below are some extracts from the 11th Northumberland Fusiliers' diary and Orders when operating in France during the time that Jack Youll was there.[2] If nothing else they give a good idea of strategy, tactics, success and failure in the field of action. They provide a vivid picture of life in the trenches and what happens when the enemy is engaged. The complexity of the operations is clear to see from the entries. This is very much the sort of daily activity which would have pre-occupied Lieutenant Jack Youll, his fellow subalterns and his men.

We can start with a number of orders marked 'Secret' and signed off by Captain R.C. Mayall (Adjutant). Here are extracts from Order No.9, dated 8 May 1915 at 10.30 pm:

1. The 68th Brigade Group will relieve the 56th Brigade Group in the OUDERDOM area on the 9th inst. The 11th NF relieving the Loyal NORTH LANCS REGT, in TORONTO CAMP.

On the night of 10th/11th the Brigade will relieve the 57th Brigade in the Right sector of the 19th Divisional Front, 11th NF probably being in reserve.

2. ADVANCE PARTY 1 NCO from A and D Companies and 1 from Transport will report to the RSM at 7.45 am and will proceed to The Headquarters 13th DLI, where they will be picked up by motor lorry and conveyed to the new area.

   The NCO of A Company will be responsible for the accommodation of Headquarters and Right Half Battalion and the NCO of D Company will be responsible for the Left Half Battalion.

3. MARCH The Battalion will parade, ready to move off, in column of route at 9.15 am. Order of march: HQ Signallers and runners, D, A, B, C, HQ, first line transport.

   Head of column at road junction K. 32. D. 4. 0. First line transport will be collected under arrangements made by the Transport Officer.

   ROUTE: Abeele, Southern Switch Road.

4. SANITATION The Orderly Officer, 2nd Lt E.G. Simons will remain at Battalion HQ until 11.00am. Each Company will leave a Sanitary Squad to ensure that their billets are left clean and latrines are filled in. They will report to the Orderly Officer at HQ at 10.45 and the Transport Officer will detail 1 GS Limbered wagon to bring on their brushes and tools.

5. DUTIES TO BE FOUND IN NEW AREA – OC A Company will detail 1 man for YMCA hut in Toronto Camp. Report at 12 noon on 10th inst.

   OC B Coy will detail 1 NCO and 6 men to report to the Divisional Bomb Officer at Bomb Store, Den Grobben Cabaret, at 12 noon on 10th inst. OC C Coy will detail 1 NCO and 3 men to report to the Divisional Bomb Officer at Dump A at TRANSPORT FARM by 12 noon on 11th inst.

6. TRANSPORT ARRANGEMENTS OCs Companies will arrange to stack all their officers' Valises, Mess Kits and men's blankets, Company Stores etc. at their Company HQ as near to the road as possible by 8.15 am. 1 L/Cpl and 2 men from each Company will be left to load.
2 motor lorries will report to the Quartermaster at HQ at 8.30am and he will be responsible for collecting the stores at the Company dumps.

Order No.10 followed soon after on 9 May:

1. The 68th Brigade will relieve the 57th on the night of 10/11th inst. in the Right Sector of 19th Divisional Front. 11th NF relieving 10th Worcesters in RAILWAY DUGOUTS. Battalion Headquarters will be at SW corner of the Bund.
2. The Battalion will parade, ready to move off at 10.15 pm on the road in the camp. Order of march: A, B, C, D, HEADQUARTERS. Entrain at BRANDHOEK at 11.00 pm. Guides meet Battalion at Railway Crossing I, 14, C, 8, 8 at 11.15 pm.
3. Defence schemes, trench stores, aeroplane photographs, maps and documents will be taken over.
4. The Signalling Officer, 1 Officer per Coy, 1 NCO from HQ and 1 per platoon will proceed into the line by daylight tomorrow. They will report at Battalion HQ at 1 pm and will proceed to RAILWAY DUGOUTS to meet guides at 3.30 pm there.
5. TRANSPORT ARRANGEMENTS. Coys will stack all Stores in/near the Guard Room as arranged by the Regimental Sergeant Major. Stores to be taken to trenches will be kept separate from those to be taken back to Transport Lines. Officers' valises and blankets will be taken up.
6. All stores to be packed by ?pm [sic].
7. Coys will take over corresponding Coys of the Worcesters.

Order No.11 came on May 13:

1. 11th NF will relieve the 13th DLI in the Left Sector on the Brigade Front on the night of 14/15th in the BUND and RAILWAY DUGOUTS.
2. B Coy relieves 13th DLI Support Coy 11th NF relieves 13th DLI Reserve Company 'A' NF relieves 13th DLI HQ will be at RUDEIN HOUSE.
3. Companies proceed via trench running on S. and ZILLEBBEB.
4. Platoon from 13th be at junction of ZILLEBEBB and VINCE at 9.30 pm.
5. ADVANCE PARTIES Advance parties consisting of 1 Officer per Coy. 6 NCOS per Coy (including I Lewis Gun NCO. & 1 R.C.O) and 1 NCO from HQ will proceed to take over the trench. Store documents, etc., to be taken over and sent to Orderly Room by 10 am 15th inst.
6. Lewis guns will be manhandled to the trenches.
7. RATIONS AND WATER Rations for HQ and 1 Coy are to be dumped at RUDEIN HOUSE thence manhandled to STAFFORD STREET. Rations for the remaining three Coys are dumped at 1.22.b.75.40i thence they are manhandled to the trenches. Major Hill will detail the necessary parties give then instructions. Drinking water to be brought up nightly in water carts to ZILLEBEBB DUMP, and distributed in petrol tins to all four Coys. Cooking water is drawn by Companies from the ZILLBBEBB STREET by a permanent party Coy. The RSM will issue the necessary instructions for this detail.

On 17 May Major C.F. (?) Wallace sent the following message on behalf of the Brigadier General, Commanding 68th Infantry Brigade:

1. I do not consider that time permits of anything like adequate preparations being made for a raid on any scale tomorrow night.

I therefore propose to send out two fighting patrols of 11th NF consisting of 1 officer and 12–15 men with the aim of identifications and doing as much damage as possible.

2. (a) No I (Right) Patrol will proceed from CRATER POST about 1.30.a.6 ¾ straight into the enemy front line opposite that post and form a block North and South.

   (b) No II (Left) will proceed from 'F' SAP about 1.30. b o. 3 ½ straight into the enemy front line at the SE end of the Sap and bomb south.

3. PROGRAMME

   ZERO

   No II patrol advances.

   Right Group will barrage 100 yards beyond enemy front line on immediate front of attack; also standing barrage on flanks of attack and CTs leading to the rear. 8 light trench mortars commence Hurricane Bombardment of enemy trenches about 1.30.[3]

   ZERO+½

   No I patrol advances

   ZERO+1

   Barrage on front line lifts to support line forming with standing barrage a box barrage around trench attacked and remaining until RA Liaison Officer with Battalion Commander orders it to cease. (see RA Programme).

4. Parties will not remain in enemy line later than ZERO+15.
5. Lewis Guns and Vickers will co-operate from our front line.

That same night Captain Mayall issued secret codes:

Code to be used on night of May 16
No. i party P
No. ii party Q
Has left our trenches A

Has entered enemy trenches V
Held up by wire C
Held up by MG fire D
Hostile barrage on No Man's Land…E
Prisoners captured F
Our casualties, wounded G
Our casualties, killed H
Has returned to our trenches K
More bombs required B
Our casualties, missing O

Numerals Z = 1 Y = 2 X = 3 W = 4 L = 5 M = 6 R = 7 S = 8 T = 9 U = 10

Order No.12 May 15:

'There are several gaps in the enemy's wire in front of our trenches, about 30 yards wide. From observation it does not appear that the enemy is holding his front line very strongly. In retaliation, a raid on the morning of the 13th and, in order for obtaining information about the unit on our immediate front, is proposed on the night of May 16th to enter the enemy's lines.

1. Lieut H.M.P. WEST and Capt. C.J.H. ADAMSON will ensure that men of the Right and Left patrols respectively have removed all identification marks before leaving our trenches.
2. It is possible that 24th Division on our left will carry out a hurricane bombardment at ZERO – 2. Great care must be taken that this is not confused with our own guns at ZERO.
3. OC Patrols will see that everyone in his parties is given his specific job before setting out: Blockers, Moppers-up, men in charge of prisoners, stretcher bearers etc.
4. ZERO hour will be at 11.00 pm instead of 10 pm.'

11th Northumberland Fusiliers Regimental War Diaries and Orders

Issued (10 copies) at 1.30 pm 17 May 1917 by runner. The copies, as the previous Orders, went to the following to ensure that every part of the Battalion who should know did know what was going on:

> 'Copy 1 HQ 68th Infantry Bde
> Copy 2 CO (Commanding officer)
> Copy 3 A Coy Copy 4 B Coy Copy 5 C Coy Copy 6 D Coy
> Copy 7 2/Lt Hunter
> Copy 8 NCO i/c Patrol
> Copy 9 Signal officers
> Copy 10 File'

On 15 May Captain Mayall sent two handwritten notes, marked 'secret'; the first to second Lieutenant Hunter; NCO B Coy; OC No. 2 Patrol, Captain Adamson; Lieutenant West:

> 'Following has been received from Brigade: some signal must be arranged from our front line to show when the party has been in the trench, say 10 minutes.
>
> 'For this purpose Lieut. West and Capt. Adamson will each arrange to fire three white parachute lights in succession from our front line. The patrols will take this as a signal to return if any are still out. These will be fired at ZERO + 10.
>
> 'I am sending herewith 3 parachute lights to OC B and C Coys (Coys have some in case these are duds).
>
> 'I am also sending tape for parties to take out with them to find their way back by.'

And then to OC C Coy:

> 'Please detail 2 stretcher bearers of your company to wait at the entrance to the dugout 10 yards South of F Sap for any casualties in

No 2 Patrol. They should be there from Zero time until the return of No 2 Patrol.

'Repeated to M.O.'

A change of plan followed on the 16th:

'With reference to para 4 of 11th NF Order No. 12 please note that your gun to be mounted in Sap G will not be required as this position will be occupied by a Vickers Gun from the M.G. Company.'

On the 17th these two reports on the raid give fascinating detail. The first is from Lieutenant West:

'To Adjutant 11th NF [Capt. Mayall]

<u>No 1 Raiding Party</u>

'The party was in position at 10.43 pm. Between 10.43 and 10.48 an enemy M.G. fired three bursts from ¼ left across our front. Our artillery opened about ¼ minutes too early. At Zero + ½ this party, led by Sgt Hand, climbed over the parapet and went straight for the enemy trench. As Sgt Hand reached the top of the parapet the Bosch put up a Very light and after that, generally speaking, kept the place lit up. The party, putting out the tape as they went, went straight ahead and disappeared into the smoke and dust caused by our barrage. A few seconds later bombs began to burst at the spot at which I expected the party to enter the enemy trench. I concluded that they had got into the trench. Our artillery appeared to lift soon after I lost sight of the party. The bombing grew more intense and at about 11.5 pm seemed to draw nearer to our trench. At about 1.6 pm the men started to return. They all came in within about 15–20 yards of where they went out and were all in by 11.9pm. I was not sure of one man at 11.10 pm so fired a white parachute light which was a dud. I then discovered that all had returned: one was wounded and seemed in 'great pain'. Several were scratched with wire.

'The accounts I have heard from the Sgt and the men are consistent. The party got close to the narrow ditch and found a gap between both rows of wire; the barrage was still on the front line, however, so they all lay down. The Sgt states that <u>all</u> his men were up with him. In about 20 seconds the artillery lifted and the party, thinking they had to 'walk over' were about to rush the trench when the Bosch threw a number of hand grenades simultaneously and continued to throw them. Our men bombed the trench but did not get in. I don't know exactly how many bombs our men threw but I would think twelve, probably more. They then retreated, the Bosch flinging bombs after them.

'The machine gun never fired a round; it must, I think, have been knocked out by our artillery as I can't imagine why it did not fire. The enemy sent up a light which split into two green ones at about 11.10 pm and another at 11.15 pm. There was no apparent result. Since our artillery ceased everything has been quiet.'

The same day the 11th Battalion Intelligence Officer reported to Captain Mayall that:

'No. 2 Party laid out in No Man's Land about 20 yards from parapet and at zero time approached enemy's line. Mr Hunter, Sgts Evans and ? [sic] reached enemy's parapet throwing bombs. The enemy was in the trench and threw bombs back and fired their rifles. Mr Hunter's party had disappeared instead of following close behind. After firing two shots and throwing bombs the officer's party returned.

'A further report will follow.

'11.38 pm.'

Here is Captain Adamson's report to Captain Mayall:

> 'Got to my post at 10.45 and found that Mr Hunter already had his men out over the Parapet. I saw them start from the Fire Step but apparently they did not all start and Mr Hunter found himself on the Boche parapet with a sergeant only. I could not see any one enter the trenches.[4]
>
> 'All Party 2 is in; two men came in before 10 minutes was up and I sent the lights up to ? [sic] and Mr Hunter and 3 others returned soon after.'

The Lieutenant Colonel Commanding 11th (S) Northumberland Fusiliers weighs in with a letter to Headquarters 68th Infantry Brigade corroborating the advance by the Right Party on the 'narrow Gap strongly held by the enemy, who were in readiness for them':

> 'The Left Party advanced at ZERO hour but owing to the darkness and the roughness of the ground, this party lost touch with one another and 2/Lt Hunter, the officer in charge, arrived at the enemy's parapet with only two men with him. The enemy immediately opened fire on them.'

With few men at his disposal, one man injured and all their bombs thrown Second Lieutenant Hunter returned to his lines at Zero + 20 to find that the rest of the party had returned on the recall signal.

Order No 14 sees B and C Coys 11th NF relieving C and D Coys 10th NF with advance parties taking over dugouts on the night of 28/29th May:

5. Coys will parade, ready to move off at 9 pm in Fighting Order with greatcoats rolled in the manner demonstrated by the RSM to Company Sergeant Majors this afternoon.
6. Each Coy will draw a cycle from HQ for use by their orderly.
7. Relief complete will be reported over the 'phone by sending the word 'HOUSE'.

11th Northumberland Fusiliers Regimental War Diaries and Orders

30 May 1917 brought order No.15, largely concerning an issue close to the heart of the troops: rations and messing:

'The 11th NF will relieve the 8th KOYLI [King's Own Yorkshire Light Infantry] in the centre Subsector of the Divisional Front on the night May 31/June 1.

'The Lewis Guns of A and D Coys will be carried on Pack Mules in rear of their respective Coys.

'The following are the arrangements for rations, water and cooking in this sector: rations for Right front company, Support Company and Battalion HQ come to JACKSON'S DUMP.

'Rations for Left front company and Reserve Company come to MANOR FARM.

'Water for Right front company, Support Coy and Btn HQ comes to JACKSON'S DUMP in water carts and is then put into petrol tins.

'Water for Left front company and Reserve Company is obtained from spring at STREAM CORNER.

'Cooking for Btn HQ, Right front company and Support coy is done in the tunnels.

'Cooking for Left front company is done at KILLEBEKE SWITCH.

'Cooking for Reserve Company is done at STREAM CORNER.

'Relief complete will be reported by sending the Company Commander's Christian name.'

We also find details regarding the make-up of HQ Btn and the various Companies along with their responsibilities:

HQ Officers
Major R.H. Gill 2/ic
Capt. G.H. Blackett, Assistant Adjutant
2nd Lieut G.B. Cowling, Lewis Gun Officer
2nd Lieut A.M. Lyone, Brigade Bombing Officer

Other staff
Orderly room staff
Signallers 4
Runners 4

B Coy Officers
Lt H.M.P. West
2nd Lt E.L.G. Clegg (hospital)
2nd Lt C.A. Hewitt (attached Brigade)
2nd Lt A.T. Exley (leave)
2nd Lt J.H. Dunn-Yarker (course)

Other ranks
Gas instructor 1
Sergeant 1
Corporal 1
Lance Corporal 1
Runner 1
Rifle bombers 4
Scouts or snipers 4
Lewis Gunners 8

D Company had a Second Lieutenant away on a wireless course and one tied up 'clearing the battlefield'. In an attack no more than two Signallers were permitted, with the rest held behind to man Command Posts, Relay Posts etc. Obviously, down to Platoon and Section level it was vital that everyone knew who was taking command if the Commander became a casualty.

Chapter 6

11th Northumberland Fusiliers: Hill 60 (Ypres) and the Battle of Messines

Jack Youll and his colleagues would not have much enjoyed their arrival at the line towards the end of July 1917, if Norman Gladden's description of his debut with the 7th Battalion is anything to go by when he arrived in September 1916:

'Even our arrival at the base camp had been welcomed by a group of jeering nondescript Tommies, no doubt down from the line, as 'more for the slaughter-house', while arrangements on the Somme were chaotic. The battle lines were fluid in more than one sense, mere ditches for the most part with little cover and hardly any shelter from the elements ... in November, the company twenty-six days in the fireard [sic] zones, with a minimum of shelter, practically no cooked food, hardly any washing or changing facilities ... the new draft was received by the battalion without ceremony or any sort of induction.'[1]

Gladden goes on to decry that they were 'made to feel that we had no rights of any sort and that rations were hard to come by, they were put on all the working parties'.

Captain Mayall in the War Diary for 9 June 1917 reveals his terrible casualties after an attack on Hill 60: Second Lieutenant (2/Lt) R.F. Bolton was wounded but later died of his wounds; 2/Lt G.T. West was also wounded and died. 160 Other ranks killed, 9 wounded and 11 missing.[2]

Hill 60 and the 1917 Battle of Messines both enjoyed fearsome reputations and 1917 became notorious as the killing grounds for numerous allied and enemy soldiers. Hill 60's record of death extended back to the very start of the war.

1914–1915

Hill 60 had been taken by the German 30th Division on 11 November 1914 during fighting against a mixed force of French and British infantry and cavalry during the First Battle of Ypres (19 October – 22 November 1914). 'Observation from the hill towards Ypres and Zillebeke was coveted by both sides for the duration of the war'.[3] Hill 60 and the vicinity were held by Saxon Infantry Regiment 105 of the 30th Division, which with the 39th Division formed XV Corps of the 4th Army, at the time of the British attack. The British 28th Division, including the 11th Northumberland Fusiliers, took over the line in February 1915, followed by 5th Division who proceeded with a reckless, if ambitious, attempt to capture the hill, despite intelligence that Hill 60 could not be held unless the nearby Caterpillar ridge was occupied at the same time. Incidentally, it emerged that Hill 60 was the only place locally that was not waterlogged and so a French 3ft × 2ft mine gallery was extended.

Troops with experience of mining from Northumberland and Wales were recruited for the mining under the auspices of tunnelling companies of the Royal Engineers (RE). In the first British operation of its kind, Royal Engineer tunnelling companies laid six mines by 10 April 1915.

Their role was to place and maintain mines below enemy lines; they might also be called on to excavate deep dugouts for billets, the digging of subways, saps (narrow trenches dug to access enemy trenches), cable trenches and underground chambers for signals and medical services. On 17 April 1915, 173rd Tunnelling Company became the first Royal Engineer tunnelling company to fire mines beneath enemy lines.

So, in spring 1915, the newly-formed 173rd Tunnelling Company was given the job of undertaking a major mining operation beneath Hill 60. In the first British offensive underground attack operation in the Ypres Salient, they laid six mines by 10 April 1915, an operation planned by

Major-General E. Bulfin, commander of the 28th Division, and continued by the 5th Division when the 28th Division was relieved. Work beneath Hill 60 began early in March and three tunnels were started towards the German line about fifty yards away, a pit first having been dug some sixteen feet deep. Almost immediately the miners came upon dead bodies and quick-lime had to be brought over to cover them. By the time the work was finished, the tunnels stretched more than 100 yards.[4] Two mines in the north were charged with 2,000 pounds of explosives each, two mines in the centre had 2,700 pound-charges and in the south one mine was packed with 500 pounds of guncotton (nitrocellulose – a replacement for gunpowder), although work on it was paused when it ran close to a German tunnel. The explosive charges were ready on 15 April and on 17 April 1915 at 19.05 the mine group was fired.

The locality was photographed from the air, which revealed German gun emplacements and entrenchments. On 16 April, British artillery was ranged by air observers onto the approaches to Hill 60, ready for the attack. British infantry began to assemble after dark and 1 Squadron Royal Flying Corps (RFC) was tasked with keeping German aircraft away from the area.

Deep mining under the German galleries beneath Hill 60 had started in late August 1915, courtesy of the 175th Tunnelling Company, which began a gallery 220 yards behind the British front line and passed 90 feet beneath the German positions.[5] The British underground works consisted of an access gallery (Berlin Tunnel) leading to two mine chambers, Hill 60 A (beneath Hill 60) and Hill 60 B (beneath the Caterpillar), to be packed with explosives and detonated at a designated time.

On 7 April at 7.05 pm, the first pair of mines were blown and the rest ten seconds later. Débris was flung almost 300ft into the air and scattered for 300yd in all directions, causing some casualties to the attacking battalions of the 13th Brigade of the 5th Division.[6] The German garrison was overwhelmed, a platoon of Saxon Infantry Regiment 105 (SIR 105) in the front line were killed, the men of the garrison who were capable of resistance were bayoneted and twenty Germans were taken prisoner for a British loss of seven casualties. However, on 1 May, the 1st Dorsets lost over 90 men to gas poisoning; 207 were brought to dressing stations, where 46 men died immediately and another twelve men died later; the battalion had only 72 survivors. The 1st Bedfords suffered similarly, having recently taken on many fresh and inexperienced replacements. Of 2,413 British casualties admitted to hospital 227 men died. The 13th Brigade casualties from 17 to 19 April were 1,362 and the 15th Brigade suffered 1,586 casualties from 1 to 7 May, out of the 5th Division total of 3,100 losses.[7]

An attempt to counter-attack was made by the 2nd Company, SIR 105, but the attack lacked coordination with the flanking companies, since the mine explosion led to the approaches now being in plain sight for the British. Some of the survivors of the 2nd Company ran back in fear that German gas cylinders, earlier placed in the front line, had been ruptured. The British began to consolidate and by 12.30 am, had dug two communication trenches to connect the new positions to the old front line.[8]

German artillery-fire gradually increased on the hill, after falling around it for some time and at around 11.10 pm four companies from IR 99, IR 143 and a machine-gun section attacked from the front and on both flanks. The attack was repulsed by British machine-gun fire, but on the right the 8th Company of SIR 105 and pioneers managed to bomb their way close to the craters and dug in under artillery-fire. Around 3.15 – 4.00 am on 18 April, three German counter-attacks began which were repelled with considerable losses; bombing parties of 2nd Company, *Pioneer Bataillon* 15, infiltrated a crater on the German left flank but were then wiped out. German high explosive and gas shells and machine-gun fire in enfilade from Zandvoorde and the Caterpillar, forced the British back to the crest, except on the right flank, where they were forced yet further back. German attacks continued all day on 18 April but at 6.00 pm, a counter-attack by two British battalions retook the hill.[9]

Before dawn on 19 April, most of the 13th Brigade was relieved by the 15th Brigade. The Germans maintained a heavy bombardment of the hill and on 20 April, after 2½ hours of 'annihilation bombardment' attacked again mainly with bombing parties, before infantry assaults were attempted at 6.30 and 8.00 pm and defeated by British machine-gun fire. German attacks continued into 21 April, by when the hill resembled 'a moonscape of overlapping shell-holes and mine craters'. The German infantry dug a jumping-off line (*Sturmausgangstellung*) and a stop line further back protected by the German artillery. The divisions of II Corps and V Corps simulated attack preparations on 21 April but on 22 April, the French 45e Division was struck by the first German gas attack of the Second Battle of Ypres and British artillery batteries were transferred northwards.[10]

The 3rd Canadian Tunnelling Company took over in April 1916 and completed the galleries, the Hill 60 mine being charged with explosives in July 1916 and the branch gallery under the Caterpillar in October.[11]

By October 1916, the mine under Hill 60 held 53,300 pounds of explosives and that under the Caterpillar 70,000 pounds despite waterlogging and the demolition by a camouflet of 200 feet of a German gallery above the British diggings, which endangered the British deep galleries.[12]

We learn from https://www.ww1battlefields.co.uk/flanders/hill-60/ that today:

> 'Hill 60 is quite a large site, and from the front and the rear, through the trees, you catch glimpses of the commanding views that made it such a prize. Looking from the front towards the road, the taller buildings of Ypres can be seen.
>
> 'The whole site is riddled with bunkers, reflecting the importance that both sides attached to this small elevated area in an otherwise largely flat landscape.'

Battle of Messines, June 1917

The division returned to the front line on 10 May near Hill 60 and started to get ready for the attack, preparations for which were clearly observed by the Germans on the higher ground who assaulted the line on 13 May. This was repulsed and attracted counter raiding by the 70th Brigade on 16 and 20 May. All the while the division's easily observed artillery attracted heavy German counter battery fire with serious casualties inflicted as a result.[13] The division was to form the left flank of the advance on a front approximately 2,000 yards wide, with its furthest advance approximately 1,400 yards deep. After the artillery bombardment and the detonation of nineteen mines on 7 June, the 69th and 70th brigades (the 69th reinforced with the 11th Northumberland Fusiliers and 12th Durham Light Infantry) advanced over the ridge and down each side of the valley on the southern flank of the Klein-Zillebeke spur, with fresh battalions leap-frogging the others when the second phase line had been reached. The new line was held until the 24th Division relieved them on 13 June.[14]

The division was aided in its endeavours by 11th, 16th, 19th, 36th, 24th, 25th, 41st, 47th and, from the 2nd ANZAC 3rd and 4th (Australian) Divisions and the New Zealand Division (Source: https://web.archive.org/web/20110719173700/http://www.ordersofbattle.darkscape.net/site/warpath/battles_ff/1917.htm).

The 1st Australian Tunnelling Company had taken over in November 1916 and maintained the mines beneath Hill 60 and the Caterpillar over the winter and months of underground fighting until June 1917, when they were fired along with the rest of the mines under Messines Ridge at the beginning of the Battle of Messines (7–14 June 1917). When the mines were detonated at 3.10 am on 7 June 1917, 990,000 pounds of explosives went off under the German positions, demolishing a large part of Hill 60 and killing around 10,000 German soldiers between Ypres and Ploegsteert.

> 'Suddenly at dawn, as a signal for all of our guns to open fire, there rose out of the dark ridge of Messines and 'Whitesheet' and that ill-famed Hill 60, enormous volumes of scarlet flame …throwing up high towers of earth and smoke all lighted by the flame, spilling over into fountains of fierce colour, so that many of our soldiers waiting for the assault were thrown to the ground. The German

troops were stunned, dazed and horror-stricken if there [*sic*] were not killed outright. Many of them lay dead in the great craters opened by the mines.'

Philip Gibbs, Holt & Holt, 2014, p. 193

The division returned to the line between 26 and 28 June in the area of Battle Wood and Mount Sorrel and began preparations for the next phase of the planned assault. During a German raid on 7 July the division's fifth VC was won by Second Lieutenant Frederick Youens. The division was relieved in the line by 24th Division by 23 July.[15]

From 3 September the division began to make preparations for its attack due east, at first along either side of the Menin Road, and then north of it, on a front 1,000 yards wide with the objective up to 2,000 yards away. The division moved into the line on 15 September. The attack began on 20 September with the 68th and 69th brigades advancing: one battalion of each brigade was to secure each of the three phase lines with the fourth as a reserve.[16] The first line was captured within the hour, the advance to the second faced resistance from pill-boxes and dug-outs as did the advance to the third. The division held this line under German artillery fire until 25 September, relieved by the 33rd and 39th divisions. In this attack the division had lost 397 killed, 1,724 wounded and 179 missing, and had captured 596 prisoners.[17]

Nevertheless, it is encouraging to know that the Battle of Messines, in which Jack Youll's battalion fought, 'proved one of the greatest tactical successes of the war'.[18] The Division enjoyed huge artillery support which sent over to the Germans 3.5 million shells while the German front line was devastated by half a million kilograms of high explosive shells.

Relief did not last long, as on 27 September the division returned to the front to reinforce the 33rd Division, which had been counterattacked after its arrival. The 69th and 70th brigades fought off further attacks, while the division artillery endured mustard gas attacks. The division left the front line on 3 October when relieved by the 5th Division, only to return on 8 October to relieve 7th Division in front of Polygon Wood.

The division was subject to heavy shelling and lost 275 killed and 954 injured before relief on 14 October.

The Battle of Polygon Wood, September 25–3 October 1917

The Battle for Polygon Wood really started in 1914 when the Germans advanced towards Polygon Wood, which at this time was defended by the British and the French. Polygon Wood in 1914 was covered with thick undergrowth which made it difficult to see your own troops, so when the British were advancing they were ordered to only use their bayonets because rifle fire might endanger other allied troops. This situation was to change considerably during later Battles for Polygon Wood when the area was flattened of all its trees and undergrowth by artillery fire.

The chief objective for the allies in 1917 was to capture the 'high ground' on either side of the Menin Road between Clapham Junction and Gheluvelt Village. The attack would come from the south near Tower Hamlet to the north east of St. Julian, a distance of six miles.

Matt Walsh tells how:

'Units of the 4th and 5th Divisions (1st Anzac Corps) were given the task of attacking and capturing the areas of Glencorse Wood – Nuns Wood (Noone Bosschen), Polygon Wood and the former German third line to the north. This offensive was to be the first time two Australian Divisions had attacked together side by side. The 4th and 5th Divisions attacked Polygon Wood on the 26th September 1917 on a 2,000 metre front.

'The attack began at 5.50 am, the enemy commander having packed his troops in the area. Opposition was encountered by the Allies and the area was not taken until 27 September 1917. The allied troops even though on level ground were up to their knees in mud and when they were in shell holes they sank up to their waists in the mud.'[19]

The Germans introduced the use of the flamethrower (*flammenwerfer*) against the British during the Battle of Polygon Wood.

It was here that Jack Youll was mentioned in despatches (MiD), although there appears to be no record of the act of bravery he did to earn the award.

A serviceman mentioned in despatches has his name appear in an official report signed off by a senior officer and sent to the high command, in which their courageous action in the face of the enemy is described. In the British Armed Forces, the despatch is published in the *London Gazette*.

Acts of valour, respect for one's enemy and observance of the rules of war, such as they were, were many and numerous in the First World War, as indeed they are in most wars. But so are their opposites: desertion and visiting atrocities on one's enemies in contravention of the very same rules of war. Nigel Cave, in his *Polygon Wood*, describes two such events which involved 12/13 Northumberland Fusiliers on the night of 2/3 October;[20] the attack was led by 3/4 Queen's with the NF 12/13 on the right flank:

> 'A gross case of treachery took place near Jupiter trench when a German officer put up his hands to surrender; Lieutenant Cooper went forward to receive it, but the German officer whipped out his revolver and shot him. Cooper has no known grave, and is commemorated on the Tyne Cot Memorial. The men who witnessed this promptly riddled the body of the German with bullets. On another occasion an inner compartment of a mebus [a specific type of German machine gun shelter used in the Hindenburg Line] opened fire after the outer garrison had surrendered so it was necessary to kill all the Germans in the post.'

And then the 12/13 took some trenches filled with German troops from the 19th Reserve Division recently posted in from Riga on the Russian front:

'The bayonet was freely used and large numbers of the fleeing enemy were shot with the rifle. Hand grenades and P[phosphorous] bombs cleared the mebus and rifle bombs the more distant shell holes. One mebus was apparently set on fire by a P bomb and burnt furiously, the whole garrison being shot as they fled or burnt to death before they could emerge.'

We also hear the story of 'a small NF soldier' who encountered a German soldier running round a mebus:

'A guttural remark to the German was met with "Nong comprez, from Riga" said the German. "To hell" said the Englishman and pushed his bayonet into his opponent's body.'

The cemetery here is reasonably large, although the bodies of many of the soldiers buried here were recovered quite some time after they had died. This explains why of 2,109 burials here only 433 are identified. Over three-quarters of the burials are unknown – men 'Known Unto God'. Most of those buried here died in 1917.

Polygon Wood, near the village of Zonnebeke, took its name from its shape on maps of the area.

In the words of https://www.ww1battlefields.co.uk/flanders/polygon-wood/:

'Polygon Wood was the scene of fighting early on in the Great War, during the First Battle of Ypres in 1914. On the 25th of October 1914 the Germans held the northern half of the wood, and 1st Irish Guards and 2nd Grenadier Guards were ordered to clear them out. During their advance here, nine of the Irish Guards were killed and four wounded by a single shell. The scene was described as "a slaughter-house". During the early hours of the next day, the two battalions, reinforced by the 3rd Coldstream Guards, attacked again.'

The small original wartime cemetery is outside the wood. There are only 107 men buried here, 89 of whom are identified. Many died in the winter of 1917/18. There was a German cemetery adjoining the British one, but those graves are long gone, although one German soldier is buried within the cemetery.

Glencorse Wood was where the First Battle of Ypres ended, on 11 November 1914. Captain Ewen Brodie of the 1st Queen's Own Cameron Highlanders was one of those killed that day, and a private memorial to him can still be seen today in Glencorse Wood. The memorial takes the form of an upright stone, with a cross carved on it and an inscription stating that the memorial stands near where Brodie was believed to have been buried. However, his body was never found. Brodie is commemorated on the Menin Gate in Ypres. The land the memorial stands on was purchased after the war by Ewen Brodie's mother, and the memorial erected in 1923. A small garden once surrounded it. It is now cared for by the CWGC.

On 28 October the division was ordered to make ready to move by rail, and on 31 October the destination was confirmed as Italy.[21]

Chapter 7

11th Northumberland Fusiliers in Italy and the British Expeditionary Force (Italy)

Although a member of the Triple Alliance, Italy did not join the Central Powers – Germany and Austria-Hungary – when the war started with Austria-Hungary's declaration of war on Serbia on 28 July 1914.

Italy had been hoping to elicit favourable terms relating to their territorial disputes from a harried Austria, but negotiations came to nothing. When these negotiations broke down, Italy was able to obtain firm promises from the Allies, which led to her declaration of war on Austria-Hungary on 23 May 1915, her break with Germany delayed until 27 August 1916. So, almost a year after the beginning of the war Italy came in on the side of the Allied Powers and took the fight against Austria-Hungary along her northern frontier, including high up in what is now the Italian Alps with their bitterly cold winters, and along the Isonzo river. The Italian army attacked time and time again and, despite winning a number of battles, suffered heavy losses and made little progress in that defender-friendly terrain. Italy was then forced to retreat in 1917 by a German-Austrian counter-offensive at the Battle of Caporetto after Russia left the war, allowing the Central Powers to pile in reinforcements to the Italian Front from the Eastern Front.

A defeated and depleted Italy needed help from her allies, France and Britain. Following the French, British forces first set foot in Italy and arrived on the Italian Front in November 1917. Youll and his 11th Battalion were soon transferred to this front. By March 1918, the 7th, 23rd and 48th (South Midland) Divisions were situated in the lofty mountains that lie north of Vicenza in the Asiago sector. The 11th

Battalion was, of course, part of the 23rd Division. The other two were the 5th and 41st, but these were re-deployed to France and Flanders before the Battle of Asiago.

It is easy to forget the impact the unforgiving terrain and brutal weather had on the conflict and on the combatants: for over three years fighting took place across Italy's northern Alpine border in Trentino, and more mountainous terrain along the Isonzo River (today Slovenia), as well as down the Adriatic coast.

Some of the First World War's harshest, most brutal fighting took place in Italy. The Alpine theatre involved men clashing at bone-piercing temperatures and amid icy storms on snow-capped, treacherous mountain peaks, in craggy, plunging valleys and ravines. In effect they were battling the elements as well as each other – the elements were a second deadly enemy that they had to contend with.

Before we go into more detail to provide a context for Jack Youll's action in Italy, here is a summary of events in the Anglo-French response to Italy's hour of need in November 1917, compiled by the Commonwealth Graves Commission in June 2018:

- Despite being allied to Germany and Austria-Hungary before the outbreak of the First World War, Italy joined the war on the side of Britain and France in May 1915.
- The first British troops to serve on the Italy Front arrived in April 1917, when heavy artillery and supporting Indian logistical units were sent to reinforce the Italian Army.
- Eleven Battles of Isonzo were fought between May 1915 and September 1917, along the Isonzo (Soca in Slovene) river valley which formed part of the border between Italy and Austro-Hungary.
- On 24 October 1917, Austro-Hungarian forces supported by German troops went on the offensive breaking the deadlock. During what became known as the Battle of Caporetto Italian forces were driven back over 100km across northern Italy to within 30km of Venice, to a line along the Piave River.

- British and French forces were rushed to Italy from the Western Front [including 11th Northumberland Fusiliers], where the Allies were engaged in the Third Battle of Ypres, to support the beleaguered Italian forces.
- In March 1918, some British, French and German troops were redeployed from Italy to the Western Front in preparation for the imminent German Spring Offensive. This left three British and three French divisions in Italy holding a section of the line around the strategically important Asiago Plateau in the foothills of the Alps.
- In June 1918, Austro-Hungarian forces launched another offensive along a broad front, some 110km from the shores of the Adriatic to Asiago Plateau.
- The timing of the Austro-Hungarian attack was known to the Allies, and their artillery opened up on the Austro-Hungarian lines 30 minutes before the beginning of the attack. Despite this bombardment Austro-Hungarian forces managed to make some gains close to the coast and across the Asiago Plateau.
- The Austro-Hungarian attack quickly faltered, Italian, French and British troops counter-attacked, driving the Austro-Hungarian forces back to their start positions along the Piave River, where many hundreds of Austro-Hungarian troops were killed trying to escape back across the river.
- Allied casualties were in the region of 85–87,000, while estimates of Austro-Hungarian losses range from between 69–118,000, wounded, missing or killed.
- The CWGC commemorates in Italy nearly 450 British Army servicemen and one Indian labourer who died during the Battle of the Piave. More than 125 are commemorated in Magnaboschi British Cemetery, over 95 in Boscon British Cemetery and more than 60 in Granezza British Cemetery, while a further 15 are named on the Giavera Memorial to the missing.

    https://www.cwgc.org/our-work/news/11-things-you-need-to-know-about-the-battle-of-the-piave-river/

The Battle of Caporetto

In short, the battle allowed Austro-Hungarian forces, reinforced by German units, to rupture the Italian front line and rout the Italian forces opposing them. The battle was at once a demonstration of the effectiveness of the use of stormtroopers and the infiltration tactics developed in part by Oskar von Hutier. The use of poison gas by the Germans also played a key role in the collapse of the Italian Second Army.[1]

The rest of the Italian Army retreated 93 miles to the Piave River; its effective strength now reduced from 1,800,000 troops down to 1,000,000 and the government of Prime Minister Paolo Boselli was now on its knees.[2]

The Germans were nothing if not prepared. In August 1917 Paul von Hindenburg and Arthur Arz von Straußenburg decided to send troops from the Eastern Front to the Isonzo Sector. Erich Ludendorff was opposed to this but was overruled.[3] Later, in September three experts from the Imperial General Staff, led by the chemist Otto Hahn, went to the Isonzo front to find a site suitable for a gas attack. They decided on attacking the quiet Caporetto sector, where a good road ran west through a mountain valley to the Venetian Plain. The Germans also sent Lieutenant General Konrad Krafft von Dellmensingen, an expert in mountain warfare, to reconnoitre the ground.[4]

On 24 October at 02.00, in the northern area of the battle (near Bovec/Plezzo) 894 metal tubes similar to Livens Projectors (*Gaswurfminen*), dug into a reverse slope, were triggered electrically to simultaneously fire canisters containing 21 imp. fl. oz. of chlorine-arsenic agent and diphosgene, enveloping the Italian trenches in a dense cloud of poison gas.[5] Knowing that their gas masks could protect them only for two hours or less, the defenders fled, but 500–600 were killed. Other parts of the valley were bombed with gas from grenades. The front was quiet until 06.00, when all the Italian wire and trenches to be attacked were bombarded by mortars.

At 06.41, 2,200 guns opened fire, many targeting the valley road along which reserves were advancing to plug the gap. At 08.00 two large mines were detonated under strong points on the heights bordering the valley and the infantry attacked. Soon they penetrated the almost undefended Italian fortifications in the valley, breaching the defensive line of the Italian Second Army between the IV and XXVII Corps. To protect the attackers' flanks, Alpine Troops infiltrated the strong points and batteries along the crests of the adjoining ridges, Matajur and Kolovrat, paying out their telephone lines as they advanced to maintain contact with their artillery. Specially-trained and equipped stormtrooper units led attacks, making use of the new German model 08/15 Maxim light machine gun, light trench mortars, mountain guns, flamethrowers and hand grenades.[6]

But it was never all one-way traffic: even before the battle, Germany was struggling to feed and supply its armies with much-needed materiel in the field. Erwin Rommel, who as a junior officer won the Pour le Mérite for his actions in the battle, often bemoaned the demands placed upon his 'poorly fed troops'.[7]

The Allied blockade of the German Empire, which the Kaiserliche Marine had been unable to break, had led to food shortages and widespread malnutrition in Germany and on the Central Powers in general. This inadequate provisioning, as well as the gruelling night marches before the Battle of Caporetto, was beginning to exact a toll on the German and Austro-Hungarian forces. However, as the territory controlled by the combined Central Powers forces expanded, so an already limited logistical capacity was overstrained. By the time the attack reached the Piave, the soldiers of the Central Powers were running perilously low on supplies and were feeling the effects of exhaustion. As the Italians began to respond to the pressure put on them, the German forces lost momentum and were once again embroiled in another round of attrition warfare.

Nevertheless, the scale and importance of the Italian defeat cannot be, and has not been underestimated: Brian R. Sullivan called Caporetto 'the greatest defeat in Italian military history'.[8] John R. Schindler wrote 'By any standard, Twelfth Isonzo [Caporetto] and its aftermath represented an unprecedented catastrophe for Italian arms'.[9] The disaster 'came as a shock' and 'triggered a search for scapegoats', culminating in a 1919

Italian military commission that investigated the causes of the debacle.[10] At Rapallo (5–7 November), a Supreme War Council was created to improve Allied military co-operation and develop a common strategy and discuss contingency plans to prevent a general collapse of the Italian front. On 5 November 1917 the Italian army withdrew from the Tagliamento Line to the Piave River. The council comprised Vittorio Emanuele Orlando the new Prime Minister and monarch, and the French and British prime ministers, Paul Painlevé (1863–1933) and David Lloyd George (1863–1945).[11]

The Italians found themselves in dire straits: only thirty-three divisions out of sixty-five remained as a viable fighting force, and they were to defend the Piave line against fifty Austro-Hungarian and German divisions supported by 4,500 guns. Painlevé and Lloyd George dispatched large reinforcements – ten divisions in total, including the 28th – but insisted that the Italian chief of staff, General Luigi Cadorna (1850–1928) be replaced with a more flexible commander. Orlando chose Armando Diaz (1861–1928), who established a more mobile force that was less constrained by rigid command structures. Italian pride had been badly shaken, but Italian soldiers seemed determined to redeem themselves.

So, Luigi Cadorna was forced to resign after the defeat.[12] Cadorna was known to have maintained poor relations with generals on his staff and by the start of the battle had sacked 217 generals, 255 colonels and 355 battalion commanders.[13]

Furthermore, Mario Morselli tells us that he was detested by his troops on account of being too harsh. Cadorna had been directing the battle some 30 miles behind the front and retreated another 160km (99m) to Padua.[14]

Italian losses at Caporetto were huge: 13,000 were killed, 30,000 wounded and 265,000–275,000 were taken prisoner. Morale was so low among the Italian troops, mainly due to Cadorna's harsh disciplinary regime, that most of these surrendered willingly. 3,152 artillery pieces, 3,000 machine guns and 1,712 mortars were lost, along with a vast quantity of other materiel. It is estimated that about 500,000 deserters disappeared. In contrast, the Austro-Hungarians and Germans sustained around 70,000 casualties.[15]

Diaz faced up to his growing manpower and materiel shortage: he rounded up the soldiers who had dispersed after Caporetto, resurrecting twenty infantry divisions and more than thirty artillery regiments by the end of February 1918. Efforts were made to restore morale and discipline – not least by increasing rations and pay – and to strengthen the Italian will to fight to the end. A special assault corps called *Arditi* was also created, as part of the Marine Brigade, highly trained and adept at fighting with knife and bomb.

Here is how events unfolded at the end of 1917, as recorded in the Battalion War Diary:

'On October 26, GHQ in France received an urgent order from London, directing Sir Douglas Haig to post with haste two Divisions to Italy in response to the devastating, almost existential, reverse suffered by the Italian Army at Caporetto and was in serious danger of collapse. As we have seen, the Supreme Inter-Allied War Council had decided on posting some British and French reserve into the Italian theatre. The 23rd and 41st Divisions, both about to be relieved on the Western Front, were selected. A further order on 8 November then expanded the force, and the 7th and 48th Divisions also prepared to move. On 14 November the 5th Division was added, making the British force in Italy five Divisions.

'The entrainment of the last units of 23rd Division was completed on 11 November 1917. It is hard for us to appreciate how powerful 'a tonic for the troops' this excursion must have been – through France, to the Riviera and Lombardy after the harrowing experiences of daily life on the Western Front.

'Unfortunately the Italian railway system completely broke down under the strain of 5 British Divisions arriving from France, and detrainment and concentration proved somewhat chaotic. However, the 23rd Division finally concentrated in the Mantua area.

Jack Youll VC. (*Republished in* Victoria Cross Heroes of World War One *by Robert Hamilton (2015, Atlantic Publishing) from the archives of Associated Newspapers*)

Thornley Colliery clearly showing how the pit dominates the village.

The Villas, the street where Jack grew up.

The Workmen's Club, Thornley.

Jack's school: the County Council School.

The gardens surrounding the Jack Youll Memorial in Thornley today.

The Jack Youll Memorial.

Gallantry information found on the Jack Youll Memorial.

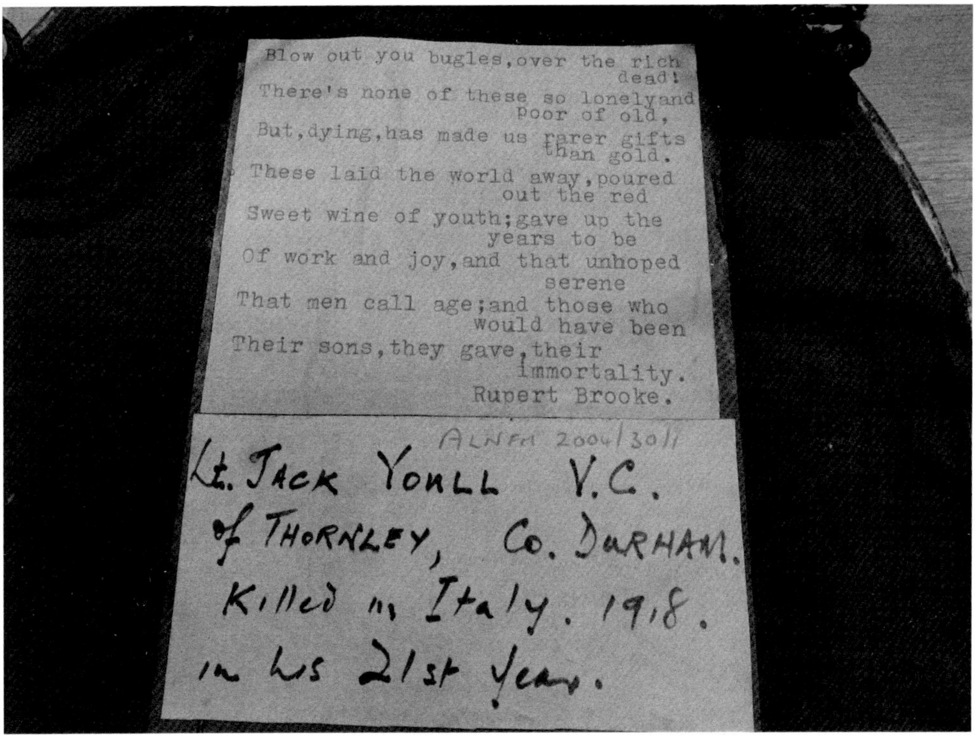

The first stanza from Rupert Brooke's *The Dead* poignantly marking Jack Youll's death. (*Courtesy of Fusiliers Museum of Northumberland https://www.northumberlandfusiliers.org.uk/*)

Smashed up German trench with corpses after the Battle of Messines Ridge. (*National Library of Scotland/ public domain*)

Carnage on Hill 60.

A jubilant group of Northumberland Fusiliers enjoying life with captured German gas masks and helmets after the Battle of St Eloi Craters, 27 March–16 April 1916, Ypres Salient. (*NAM 1998-06-181-7*)

Troops of the 1/5th Battalion, Northumberland Fusiliers waiting their turn for a haircut, Toutencourt, October 1916. Note that the second man in the queue is wearing a German cap. (*IWM Q1366*)

Italian troops salvaging what they can after a trench takes a direct hit.

Fighting high up in the mountains.

Newspaper cutting citing Jack Youll's brave action at Polygon Wood, which won him a mention in despatches. (The Graphic, *27 July 1918* – *www. ukphotoarchive.org.uk/the-graphic-portraits-xyz/h75719F22#h75719f22*)

A NEW V.C.

Lieut. J. Scott Youll, one of the latest recipients of the V.C., did excellent work at Polygon Wood, gained the highest honour and also the Italian silver medal for valour.

The watch presented to Jack Youll by the people of Thornley. (*Courtesy of Fusiliers Museum of Northumberland*)

Second Lieutenant Jack Youll VC.

A proud Jack Youll showing off his VC to a comrade. (*https://www.ukphotoarchive. org.uk/ww1victoriacrossrecipients/ h814671A8#h814671a8*)

The cigarette case presented to Jack Youll by the people of Thornley. (*Courtesy of Fusiliers Museum of Northumberland*)

'It was agreed at a high command meeting on 14 November to move the 23rd and 41st Divisions immediately into the front line in the Vicenza area, as soon as the Italians could provide road and billeting facilities, which could not happen before the 19th, the date on which the march to the new front began in perishingly cold weather from Mantua towards Legnano. The new front was on the River Brenta. On 28 November, the two Divisions were moved again, the 23rd going via Castelfranco and Montebelluna to the front lines of the Montello Sector where the 23rd Division remained until March 1918. Things were relatively quiet through the savage winter although regular enemy shellfire continued.'[16]

The War Diary speaks eloquently of the calibre of the forces the 11th Battalion was up against in an Austrian infantry attack on 15 June which advanced:

'Headed by Assault Troops and bombers and machine gunners and Flammenwerfen [they] were the only dangerous element and [they] showed great gallantry and enterprise.'

As Ball points out, 'These are storm troop tactics cascaded from the German Army'.[17]

Private Norman Gladden has much in common with Jack Youll, so the detailed account he gives in *Across the Piave* is particularly important to us. We can let him introduce himself:

'I was not deluded by the romantic visions of the heroic nature of war that swept across Europe at the outbreak ... Towards the end of 1915 I attested, and took the King's shilling under the Derby scheme, the State's last attempt to meet the war's manpower needs without conscription ... I was recalled to the colours, as the scheme provided, the following May, just three months before the then official enlistment age of 19; and served with the 2/1 Hertfordshires at Hertford, Newmarket and Harrogate. With the speeding up of drafting following the great Somme losses, my training was compressed to an impossibly short four months and I went abroad with my battalion's second draft, to join the 7th Northumberland Fusiliers in the 50th Division on the Somme, where, by the end of the year, I had been converted into an old sweat, taken part in the battles for Le Sars and the Butte de Warlencourt, seen my dearest pal fatally wounded, contracted trench feet through constant immersion and returned a casualty to Blighty, via No 6 General Hospital at Rouen, where I arrived on Christmas morning. After kind treatment by the military hospital services and people of Cardiff and Bridgend, and much less sympathetic re-training at the regiment's depot at Catterick, I returned to France on 5 May 1917 to join the 11th Northumberland Fusiliers in the 23rd Division, with which I served with only one home leave, and that after the armistice, until my discharge early in 1919.'

Gladden, soon to be part of a Lewis gun team, points out some interesting cultural and military idiosyncrasies which set the Italians and Austrians apart from anything the Battalion had experienced on the Western Front.[18] Referring to handovers and the daily routine, Gladden tells us in what could be termed a description of war by fiesta and siesta:

'In some cases, it is said, barrels of wine were handed over as trench stores! The Official History throws an interesting sidelight on a somewhat slap-happy way of conducting war, even after Caporetto. Another difficulty experienced in cooperating with the Italians was their habit of closing down from 12 to 3 pm every afternoon for the midday meal and rest, a habit continued even when the war was not going too well for them; as the Austrians knocked off at 11.30 am for a couple of hours the cause did not suffer. As noon approached Italian officers very obviously became uneasy and wanted to stop any work in hand. All this would soon be changed.'

Improvisation was essential in the face of unpredictable rations and an underwhelming cookhouse. Gladden regales us, around 12 January 1918, with the simple pleasure in being able to spend one's pay on what must have felt like little luxuries:[19]

> 'The continual bustle of transports and working parties that had been the normal accompaniment of war on the Western Front, was entirely absent here. Down the road the West Yorkshires had opened a canteen, which was available to all. Their display of good things right in the line took our breath away. Notes of some purchases which I made show the following items and prices paid (expressed in lire, then worth sixpence):
>
> Small tin of salmon 2.30
> Boot polish 0.85
> Sardines, 2.00
> Chocolate (small packet), 2.20
> Erasmic soap, 1.00
> Collins 9d novel (cloth bound), 3.30'

Erasmic soap was shaving soap, probably in stick form then. It is still selling today: 'loved by men for over 13 decades' goes the sales pitch.

The Evils of Drink
The evils of drink and of supposedly 'evil' women are all too familiar in combat life, and the relative potency of Italian wine compared to French had been made abundantly clear, as described by a pious Gladden:[20]

> 'Warnings on the potency of the local *vino rosso* had gone unheeded, and the wine shops were reaping a rich harvest in lire. That same night … At least half the company had rolled home drunk. Unfortunately, this included the Lewis gun section, except for Tom and me, who had opted out. Corporal Goffee, old campaigner as he was, had

found no difficulty in drinking the others under the table. Under his leadership as host for the occasion they had gone with the fixed intention of having a booze-up. The results must have exceeded their expectations. During the night most of our companions were as sick as dogs, and the following morning our room was in an indescribable state. With the fetid atmosphere of the small room, our blankets soiled or threatened on all sides by the expelled half consumed wine, my companions white-faced and groaning with internal discomfort, I thought when I awoke from a fitful slumber that I had landed in some special section of Dante's Inferno. To throw open doors and windows wide, to fling on one's clothes, and to flee into the open air was an immediate necessity to avoid joining the repentant revellers in their particular revulsions. At that moment it was not easy to avoid a feeling of self-righteousness at this picture of normal gentlemen driven by hopeless, deadly monotony to seek diversion at the price of becoming like senseless beasts, wallowing in their own filth. In retrospective extenuation, I can write that this particular group did not frequently indulge themselves in this way, nor do I recollect that they ever showed resentment to those of us who chose to enjoy ourselves in our own way.'

Wayward WAACS

We find Gladden again in what may be described as 'prim mode' when he describes the shenanigans allegedly caused by an influx of women into areas behind the lines. Obviously, he cannot be expected to have seen at that point what sterling work these women soldiers and other agencies did for the British war effort throughout the war.[21] Even taking into account the vast gulf between cultures and attitudes towards permissiveness then and now, it has to be said that much if not all of this was based on hearsay and speculation. Fake news 1916 style?

'As in the previous year there had been trouble at the base at Etaples, even rioting; the worm turning at last! Members of the women's corps, the WAAC and other units, had been arriving in force. In the early days their sanitary arrangements had been very primitive. The wash-houses were exposed, as so often our own were. In our case it did not matter, but now in the case of the female the publicity was different – men were not slow in availing themselves of the opportunity offered. Apart from this natural inclination of the male to improve the shining hour, most of us were shocked by all this. After all we had not yet 'progressed', if that is the proper word, very far from Victorian ideas of propriety. The general opinion at the time was that the sending of women to share these conditions was quite unnecessary, so long as there were males at the base fit enough for the auxiliary tasks, and there was also the feeling that there were still plenty of male slackers to be combed out at home. Already the tale was going round that the authorities had other notions in sending over women to play their part. It was felt that a little more female company would help to keep up morale. We were certainly not impressed by this line of reasoning for we could see no reason why the morale of the base wallahs should require this special consideration. However, we did realise that in the minds of the people at home there was no distinction between the base and the line troops. As an example of the situation that had developed, one informant told us that when air raid warnings came during the night, and this, he said, happened rather more frequently than appeared to be strictly necessary, it was the practice to allow the troops to break camp and bivouac in the fields around. On these occasions he had seen Tommies and WAACs pairing under the same blankets. The authorities turned a blind eye to these goings on, or appeared to do so, for in the darkness things could happen without anyone becoming too much concerned. We all took a very poor view of these reports, perhaps largely because we were dogs in the manger too far away to share in the frolics. I do not know how far it was official policy to encourage fraternisation among the lower orders in this way, with the object of meeting natural needs, keeping up morale and winning the war, but I think there must have been something in it during both the major wars, contributory factors in the changes in moral attitudes and sex relations which have undoubtedly been taking place during the present century. Other stories centred on goings on at a rest camp in Marseilles and on an army hospital there for venereal diseases, in which there was no dearth of cases. Mixed with definite authentic news of retreats on the Western Front, these other tales helped to build up a very depressing picture, particularly at a time when we found enough personal discomfort in our immediate surroundings.'

However, an influx of a very different kind did meet with approval: the arrival of American troops with the promise of many more to come was seen as welcome news: Gladden describes how one of the Battalion's NCOs, who had been attached to an American group for a few days, told how one Northumberland Fusilier battalion had been relieved by our new allies. They were, he said, 'of fine physique (contrasting particularly with our dwindling standards of physical fitness), well-equipped and filled with a superb self-confidence and eagerness to get at the Germans'. Even so, Gladden and his comrades cannot resist a swipe and a good laugh at the Americans' lack of battle experience and, perhaps, naivety at this early stage of their war.[22]

We will, of course, never know now whether Jack Youll imbibed the demon drink to excess (many soldiers did, if only to break the monotony and hide their fear) or what he thought about WAACs and soldiers having a good time (who knows, it may be their last chance); we don't know if he knew that tobacco supplies were low and substituted by *ersatz* tea leaves – our clean living Lewis gunner (Gladden) smugly congratulates himself on being 'doubly fortunate in being a non-smoker' adding that it was 'not pleasant to witness the tortures of those who were in the grip of this craving'. One hopes, however, that Jack Youll was able to avail himself of the service the stretcher bearers were ordered to offer – rubbing oil into the soldiers' feet in a bid to stave off the ravages of frostbite.[23]

The Spanish Flu

No account of the Great War can be complete without at least a nod to that great 1918 pandemic which crossed frontiers and savaged all armies indiscriminately, untroubled by nationalism of any kind. Its morbid effect on morale, mortality and physical health generally was, of course, profound, as was its impact on strategy and tactics throughout all adversaries from the highest echelons to the 'poor bloody infantry'.

The 1918–1920 Spanish Flu (H1N1 influenza A virus) pandemic was one of the most lethal natural disasters ever, infecting an estimated 500 million people across the globe (about a third of the world's population at the time – in four successive waves) and claiming between 50 and 100 million lives. To put its brutal rapacity into some kind of context, if the COVID 19 pandemic of the early 2020s had killed at the same rate as the 1918 pandemic, there would have been more than 200 million deaths globally rather than the accepted 7 million according to the WHO (as of June 2025: https://data.who.int/dashboards/covid19/deaths?n=o). This 1918 influenza pandemic has been described as 'the greatest medical holocaust in history' and is estimated to have killed in a single year more people than the Black Death killed in four years from 1347 to 1351. Some historians and people who write about history forget just what an impact it had on aspects of the war.

> 'It stalked into camp
> when the day was damp
> And chilly and cold.
> It crept by the guards
> And murdered my pards
> With a hand that was clammy and bony and bold;
> And its breath was icy and mouldy and dank,
> And it killed so speedy
> And gloatingly greedy
> That it took away men from each company rank.'
>
> *From* The Flu *by Private Josh Lee, 1919*

An article by Peter C. Wever and Leo van Bergen (2014) gives an interesting perspective on the effects of the pandemic on First World War combat.

The setting is the Meuse-Argonne offensive, a decisive battle during the war, which remains the largest frontline commitment in American military history involving 1.2 million US troops. With over 26,000 deaths among American soldiers, the offensive is considered 'America's deadliest battle'. Despite these prodigious numbers the authors remind us that 'It has been stated, however, that more Americans were buried in France because of 1918 pandemic influenza than of enemy fire'.[24] The offensive coincided with the highly fatal second wave of the influenza pandemic which ran its deadly course over about eight weeks, from 15 September to 15 November 1918. Wever and van Bergen reveal how:

> 'In Europe and in US Army training camps, 1918 pandemic influenza killed around 45,000 American soldiers making it questionable which battle should be regarded 'America's deadliest'. The origin of the influenza pandemic has been inextricably linked with the men who occupied the military camps and trenches during the First World War. The disease had a profound impact, both for the military apparatus and for the individual soldier. It struck all the armies and might have claimed toward 100,000 fatalities among soldiers overall during the conflict while rendering millions ineffective.'[25]

Indeed, the highest morbidity rate was found among the Americans as the disease infected 26 per cent of the US Army, over one million men. In comparison, the German army recorded over 700,000 cases of influenza, while the British Expeditionary Forces (BEF) listed 313,000 cases in 1918 in France.[26]

There are a number of claims as to its origin:

- Some contend that it started in a British military base at Étaples, a base crowded with soldiers near sea marshes with lots of migratory birds, many farms nearby with pigs, ducks, and geese reserved as food for soldiers, and a storage facility for mutagenic war gases. These conditions might have contributed to an outbreak of acute respiratory infection between December 1916 and March 1917 which clinically resembled 1918 pandemic influenza.

- Others say that the origin can be traced to Indochinese soldiers from Vietnam, Laos, and Cambodia fighting in France among which several epidemics of acute respiratory infections were noted (Annamite pneumonia).
- The best candidate for this dubious privilege is Camp Funston, a US Army training camp in Kansas, where in March 1918 Chinese contract workers at the camp presented with influenza. Soon, the disease spread across the camp requiring hospitalization of over 1,100 soldiers within three weeks, besides thousands more receiving treatment at infirmaries around the camp. From Camp Funston the influenza jumped to other US Army training camps and travelled to Europe aboard troop ships. In all, 11.8 per cent (143,986) of over 1.2 million men in US Army training camps were hospitalised for respiratory illness in March-May 1918.

Siegfried Sassoon described the impact of the disease. 'The influenza epidemic defied all operation orders of the Divisional staff, and during the latter part of June more than half the men in our brigade were too ill to leave their billets.'[27]

Likewise, German General Erich Ludendorff said 'Influenza was rampant …It was a grievous business having to listen every morning to the chiefs of staffs' recital of the number of influenza cases, and their complaints about the weakness of their troops if the English attacked again.'[28]

The super-lethal second wave struck in August and September 1918, and on 6 October:

'Influenza and pneumonia ... increased by thousands of cases. Case mortality of pneumonia, 32 per cent, even further increasing to 45.3 per cent in the week of 11 October. In that week, during the height of the Meuse-Argonne offensive, the highest number of deaths from influenza in the AEF was reached with 1,451 reported fatalities.'

By 23 October, there were 20,000 more patients than normal bed capacity in the AEF.

Captain Geoffrey Keynes of the Royal Army Medical Corps (RAMC) would never forget the sight of the mortuary tents at Bohain, France. 'There were rows of corpses, absolutely *rows* of them, hundreds of them, dying from something quite different. It was a ghastly sight, to see them lying there dead of something I didn't have the treatment for.'

Gladden first mentions the virus around 22 May 1918, where he records the first mention of the fever having broken out among the 23rd Division with cases hospitalised. By 10 June, however, the *Official History* reports the disease to be receding, although cases were diagnosed in the 11th Battalion. There is no evidence either way that Jack Youll caught Spanish Flu, but he was obviously affected by it indirectly, as were all his battalion comrades, if only by the depletion of the ranks. Gladdon, however, may well have caught it:[29]

'I developed a bad cold, a misfortune to which I had never been particularly subject. No doubt it was something more than a cold, although at the initial stages I did not connect it with the epidemic that was raging ... My head was thick; I was without energy and no doubt had a touch of the flu. More cases had gone down that morning.'

He describes the soaking and freezing trench he slept in one night as 'not very good treatment for flu!', and adds that a planned 'stunt against the enemy' was 'a physical impossibility with hundreds going down with the epidemic. We heard that the hospitals behind the lines were already filled to overflowing'.

On 13 June after returning from the night's patrol there was a medical parade at which 'a further half-dozen of the platoon reported sick. I had half a mind to join them, for I was feeling really ill'. Gladden's stoicism stems partly from a 'strong disinclination to do anything that might be construed as an attempt to evade front line duty. Those others certainly appeared to be no worse than I was'. No one was going to accuse him of 'slacking'; what could not have occurred to him was the good chance that he was, by not quarantining, spreading the disease – infection control and epidemiology were in their infancy to the layperson in the summer of 1918.

Chapter 8

The Battle of Asiago, 15–23 June

The Diary continued with the information that with winter more or less over, on 12 March 1918 the Division received orders to get ready for a move. The British were to take over a section of the front on the Asiago Plateau, a mountainous region with peaks ranging from 4,500 to 5,000 feet and zigzagging 1-in-10 roads to the north of Vicenza still snow-covered. So special preparations in terms of equipment, signalling methods and the like were required. Relieved on 14 March by Italian units, the Division marched to an area east of Vicenza and then by lorry to occupy the line on 27 March, taking over from the Italian 12th Division.

Trench warfare continued with its usual horrors and perils. At one point preparations were made for an offensive, but this was cancelled after intelligence was received from enemy deserters regarding an impending Austrian offensive on the Lower Piave.

Meanwhile, the night of 1/2 June saw the Battalion raid three houses in front of the Austrian line, killing at least ten of the enemy and taking two prisoners.

Two weeks later on 15 June, the Austrian 11th Army struck the first blow in what was henceforth called the Battle of Asiago when they attacked the British 23rd and 48th Divisions' positions on the Asiago Plateau, with about four and a half divisions. The enemy's artillery attack included a deadly cocktail of gas, shrapnel, high explosive and even armour-piercing shells, fired from every calibre of gun, with the assault on the British sector described by Lieutenant General Cavan as a 'short but violent bombardment'. The British front was being held by the 23rd and 48th Divisions, both seriously depleted due to lack of reinforcements and cases of influenza; each was holding 4,000 yards (2.27 miles) of line. The 11th Northumberland Fusiliers at this time had a trench strength of about 500 men and were in position near a trench called the Boscon Switch.

Intelligence about the impending attack was good and at 3 am on 15 June, a heavy bombardment including gas opened along the entire British front and battery position. Fortunately, the fire was neither registered nor accurate, but did have its own serious hazards, bringing trees down and sending wood and large rock splinters flying through the air. The enemy artillery signalling lines were soon out of action. British counter-battery response opened up at 5 am and was very effective all day long.

The Austrian infantry attack opened at 7 am, and the battle soon broke in the mist and wooded country into fragmented skirmishes, with hand to hand fighting. The 23rd Division lost a little ground at the flanks but recovered it during the day. The front of the 48th Division was broken at several places but again this was recovered by early on the 16th.

Norman Gladden's vivid account shows very clearly what the British were up against:[1]

'Guns were firing out in front, actually out in front! Flashes lit up the hills on the far side of the plateau and a roar of artillery rolled along the entire front. A crescendo of sound, and then the storm burst upon us. Screaming shells rushed to earth amidst the wire, and behind us, or further over in the woods. Lumps of rock were hurled about by the explosions. The trench soon became swathed in a cloud of acrid smoke … Over my shoulder, as I crouched, I could see the bursts of incendiary shells, and, as I watched, a tremendous flame rose up as some of the trees caught fire. The flames leapt up like gigantic red seas beating against a breakwater and glowed through the gaunt trees which banked up the hillside above us. It was a terrifying but magnificent sight. I rejoined the section breathless but unhurt.

'The bombardment continued. Heavy shells streamed over 119 like express trains, to burst in the further recesses of the hills, with a shattering roar which could be heard even above the general bombardment. Cries for stretcher-bearers began to arise on our left, and from time to time word was passed along that some poor devil was wounded or "had got the knock". Who would be next?'

And then came the dreaded gas:

'A cry of "Gas!" jerked me out of my musings, and the acrid flames of a shell-burst close by caused me to imagine that the gas was already upon us. I adjusted my box respirator excitedly, taking more time than was usual on parade and, my companions having done likewise, we crouched round in our weird garb puffing through our rubber mouthpieces and looking like other-world creatures from a novel by H.G. Wells.

'One man made a sorry mess of adjusting his helmet, got a whiff of gas and had to be taken to higher ground further up the trench to await his chance of getting out. The bombardment, owing no doubt to the use of gas shells, appeared at this juncture to become less severe. No news had come up from the valley since the alarm had sounded and two of us went along to regain contact.'

This is the sort of unforgettable horror story Wilfred Owen described when he wrote:

> 'An ecstasy of fumbling
> Fitting the clumsy helmets just in time,
> But someone still was yelling out and stumbling
> And flound'ring like a man in fire or lime.
> Dim through the misty panes and thick green light,
> As under a green sea, I saw him drowning.
> In all my dreams before my helpless sight,
> He plunges at me, guttering, choking, drowning.'
> *Wilfred Owen, Dulce et Decorum Est, 1921 ll 9–16*

The Battle of Asiago, 15–23 June   77

The War Diary reveals that British patrols were sent out from the 11th Northumberland Fusiliers to garner intelligence regarding enemy movements, in the belief that the Austrians were confused and demoralised, but they ran soon into resistance that suggested that this was far from the case. In one such patrol, a young officer of the 11th Northumberland Fusiliers demonstrated prodigious bravery that led to an award of the Victoria Cross. By the time the fighting died down, the 11th Battalion had suffered 104 casualties – amounting to one-fifth of the total of casualties suffered by the whole Division. The patrols managed to slow the attacks on the land in front of the battalion as well as the 12th (S) Durham Light Infantry (Pioneers). The Brigade War Diary takes up the story:

'At *5.00 am* a message had been received from one of those patrols saying they had dug in and were waiting for things to quieten down …

'*8.40 am*: the 11th NF (Left Front) reported that the 48th Division on their left had been driven back and the parties of the enemy had been seen advancing through the woods. A Left Defensive Flank was formed and was heavily engaged. The situation here was not satisfactory owing to the retirement of the 1/4th TE Oxford and Buckinghamshire Light Infantry Regiment and it was principally about this time that the 11th NF under Major Gill, particularly distinguished themselves. Their numerous heroic efforts are too numerous to mention here but that of Lieut. Youll who had brought in his patrol at 5.00am is an example. The officer behaved magnificently and by establishing a post on the Romcalto Road where it cut the 48th Divisional Front repeatedly restored the situation for short periods, and materially assisting in the capture of large parties of the enemy by cutting off their retreat, before this he had killed the team of an enemy machine gun, and used this gun with another one captured against the Austrians.

'The Assault Troops in this operation were the only dangerous element and these showed great gallantry and enterprise in such things as climbing trees and attempting to enfilade our trenches from the portion of the 48th Divisional Front they had captured.

'*12.30 pm* ... the situation on the left was now reported restored, the British line being still intact and a defensive flank composed of the reinforcing Company of the 10th NF thrown back in touch with the 48th Division. In this operation the enemy had very nearly reached Battalion HQ the personnel of which turned out in defence.'

The brigade's ammunition dumps were lost, but were regained later in the day.

By 7.10 pm the 11th NF on the left who had maintained their position against frontal and flank attacks all day had suffered heavily, and having already two companies of the 10th NF under their orders Major Gill decided to relieve them by the HQ and the remaining two companies of the 10th NF. This relief was completed before midnight 15/16 June when the 11th NF returned to the Second Line behind the Right Battalion Front, one company being in Brigade Reserve at Monte Torle. Two companies of the 8th Yorks Regiment from the Reserve brigade that had been placed under Major Gill's command were sent, one to the second line behind the Left Battalion, and one in Brigade Reserve at Monte Torle.

By 9.00 am on the following day the 10th Northumberland Fusiliers reported to HQ that the 48th Division had managed to retake their front line and the situation was completely restored. The 11th Battalion had sustained 104 casualties. For his role in the operations Lieutenant Youll was recommended for a VC ...

According to Cavan, things were tougher for the 48th Division. He reported that:

'Austro-Hungarian stormtroopers managed to capture the British frontline trench on the 15th of June and push the 48th Division back some 1,000 yards.

'However, the ground behind the frontline had been prepared well. A series of switches and slip trenches had been dug, allowing the 48th to fall back into defendable positions along their line.

'On the morning of the 16th, the 48th Division launched a ferocious counterattack. The Austro-Hungarian troops were driven back from the pocket they were occupying. By 9.00 am, the 48th Division was back in its starting position.'[2]

There followed a major push by the British. Cavan reported:

'Acting with great vigour during the 16th, both divisions took advantage of the disorder in the enemy's ranks, and temporarily occupied certain posts in the Asiago Plateau without much opposition. Several hundred prisoners and many machine guns and two mountain howitzers were brought back in broad daylight without interference.

'As soon as "No Man's Land" had been fully cleared of the enemy we withdrew to our original line. The enemy suffered very heavy losses in their unsuccessful attack. In addition, we captured 1,060 prisoners, 7 mountain guns, 72 machine guns, 20 *flammenwerfer* (flamethrowers), and one trench mortar.'

Straußenburg's Army Group Commanders, Conrad von Hötzendorf (the former Austro-Hungarian Chief of Staff) and Svetozar Boroević von Bojna, both wanted to make a decisive assault against the Italians, but could not agree on the location of the attack. Boroević struck first, moving southwards along the Adriatic coast and in the middle of the River Piave. The Austro-Hungarians crossed the Piave, capturing a bridgehead 15 miles wide and 5 miles deep despite heavy Italian resistance: Diaz deployed his reserves against the Austrians' bridgehead. The Italians assailed the Austrian pontoons with aircraft and artillery fire. Nine days later, Boroević ordered the retreat across the river to avoid his bridgeheads being wiped out.

The Japanese writer Harukichi Shimoi recalls:

'Thick bursts all around me, very close. I saw many who died and who were wounded. I will never forget those two days. A young soldier fell wounded; a piece of shrapnel had entered his right leg, another under the right eye and another in the right ear …I approached him and bandaging his leg, I took him on my shoulders and, comforting and encouraging him, I took him to the dressing station. He, feeling bloody, asked me in a low voice for my name. I told him simply: "A Japanese, a lover of Italy." What does it matter to hear Shimoi's name? I'd be happier to let him know that the shoulders of a Japanese had given him support!'[3]

The Austrian infantry assault, comprising four-and-a-half regiments, was formidable, and by 08.00 am on 15 June it had broken through the British line. A two Division British line that was seriously undermanned and afflicted by an influenza epidemic was responsible for 4,000 yards of line – 2.27 miles. This prompted the 11th Northumberland Fusiliers (about 500 men strong) to form a defensive flank near a trench called the Boscon Switch, while at the same time sending out patrols to gather intelligence that would enable them to institute tactics to keep the Austrians at bay.

Over the following days Boroević resumed the attack, but the artillery barrage smashed many of the river's bridges; consequently, the Austro-Hungarian formations that had crossed the river were unable to receive reinforcement and supplies. To make things worse still, the swollen Piave isolated many units on the west bank of the river, rendering them easy prey for the Italian fire and many Austro-Hungarian soldiers drowned while trying to reach the east bank.[4] On 19 June, Diaz counter-attacked and hit Boroević's flank, inflicting heavy casualties.

On 15 June, Conrad attacked along the Italian lines west of Boroević on the Asiago Plateau with the objective of capturing Vicenza. His forces gained some ground, but met stiff resistance from Italian units, taking 40,000 more casualties. In the aftermath, Boroević was particularly critical of Conrad who, after the complete failure of the first attack, opted to continue the assaults but on a smaller scale, rather than send reinforcements to the Piave sector.[5]

Lacking supplies and facing attacks by armoured units, the Austro-Hungarians were ordered to retreat by Emperor Karl, who had taken personal command on 20 June. Three days later, the Italians had recaptured all the lost territory on the southern bank of the Piave and that was the end of the battle.

In the final analysis this was a decisive victory for the Italian Army over the Austro-Hungarian Empire, although at first its full significance was not appreciated in Italy. Yet Erich Ludendorff, on hearing the bad news, said he 'had the sensation of defeat for the first time'.[6] General Paul von Hindenburg (1847–1934) also deemed it to be the end of any Austrian threat to Italy. It would soon become clear that the lost battle was in fact the beginning of the end for the once mighty Austro-Hungarian Empire. The battle also signalled the beginning of the end for the Imperial-Royal Army as an effective fighting force, which was finished off at the Battle of Vittorio Veneto some four months later.

Among its multiple appearances subsequently in various media perhaps the most famous is the 1932 film adaption of Hemingway's *A Farewell to Arms* in which Frederic Henry takes a leg wound just as the 18-year-old ambulance driver Hemingway did on 8 July. Hemingway was knocked unconscious during an Austrian mortar attack. Shrapnel cut into his legs. Two Italian soldiers standing with Hemingway were killed.

Military Strength of the Belligerents and Casualties

The Allies
57 divisions:[7]

(ITALY)	900,000 in 52 divisions
(BRITAIN)	~40,000 in 3 divisions
(FRANCE)	25,000 in 2 divisions

Total: 965,000

5,650 guns
1,570 mortars
676 aircraft

Casualties: 87,181:
8,396 dead
30,603 wounded
48,182 captured

Austria-Hungary
946,000
6,833 artillery pieces

Casualties: 118,042[8]
11,643 dead
80,852 wounded
25,547 captured

On July 15 Norman Gladden writes:[9]

> 'It was still unmistakeably a battlefield, littered with the debris of war and so different in appearance from the many other quiet forest fringes through which our line meandered. We were soon scrounging for souvenirs among the litter. I salvaged a short blood-stained Austrian bayonet, which I managed to hold on to throughout the rest of the campaign and have before me on the desk at this moment. I remember subjecting it to a good deal of cleansing at the time but the stain still shows.'

The extract reveals just how common, and acceptable, post-battle souvenir hunting was. Some twenty-five years later the author's father, Gunner Eric Chrystal, was in late 1943 with 1st Air Landing Light Regiment working their way up through the mountains of southern-central Italy, when he too paused to salvage a souvenir: in this case a German Second World War bayonet in its scabbard. By coincidence, 'I have [it] before me on the desk' as I write; unlike Norman Gladden's trophy, it requires no cleansing as it was, and still is, in pristine condition, the blade gleaming as if to belie its murderous purpose. It has never needed cleaning, probably because it is marked 'Solingen Rostfrei' – Germany's answer to Sheffield.[10]

Chapter 9

Jack Youll's VC Action

Jack Youll was involved in two major and decisive battles in Italy in 1918, one of which saw him win the Victoria Cross and the Italian Silver medal for valour; the other was where he was killed in action.

It was while serving in Italy on attachment with the 11th (Service) Battalion, Northumberland Fusiliers, that Youll became the first officer in the Northumberland Fusiliers to win the VC since the Siege of Lucknow – during the Indian Mutiny (1857–1858) – more than half a century earlier.

As noted, on 15 June 1918, encouraged by the effective withdrawal of Russia and Romania from the war, the Austrians launched an offensive on the Italian Front, usually known as the Third Battle of the Piave. The British Sector of the Front, which ran westwards from south of Asiago to north of Cesuna, was held in the east by the 23rd Division and in the west by the 48th. 11th Battalion The Northumberland Fusiliers was on the left flank of the 23rd Division, effectively in the centre of the British line, south of Roncalto. The Austrian attack made a deep impact on the battalion, which was forced back and formed a defensive flank towards the Boscon Switch, sending out patrols to gather information and harass the Austrians.

One of these patrols was led by Temporary Second Lieutenant J.S. Youll.

The London Gazette of Thursday 25 July 1918 described Jack Youll's singular courage that day. The citation says it all:

> 'His Majesty the KING has been graciously pleased to approve of the award of the Victoria Cross to the undermentioned Officers …

'For most conspicuous bravery and devotion to duty during enemy attacks when in command of a patrol which came under the hostile barrage. Sending his men back to safety, he remained to observe the situation. Unable subsequently to rejoin his company, 2nd Lieutenant Youll reported to a neighbouring unit, and when the enemy attacked he maintained his position with several men of different units until the troops on his left had given way and an enemy machine gun had opened fire from behind him. He rushed the gun and, having himself killed most of the team, opened fire on the enemy with the captured gun, inflicting heavy casualties. Then, finding that the enemy had gained a footing in a portion of the front line, he organised and carried out with a few men three separate counterattacks. On each occasion he drove back the enemy, but was unable to maintain his position by reason of reverse fire. "Throughout the fighting his complete disregard of personal safety and very gallant leading set a magnificent example to all"'.[1]

Due to the arrival of Allied reinforcements later in the day, the Austrian offensive was repelled, although the 11th Northumberland Fusiliers suffered casualties amounting to a fifth of its strength.

Youll, who was single, received his VC from King George V at an investiture at Buckingham Palace on 4 September 1918.

He was one of just eight men from County Durham to receive the VC in the Great War.[2] This is how Norman Gladden generously describes the achievement from the front line:

'There was an interesting event on 30 July, when the battalion paraded with great ceremony to witness the presentation of the Victoria Cross to 2nd Lieutenant Youll of 'C' Company, whose exploit at the Battle of Asiago has already been mentioned [not found]. This was a great honour to the battalion, and ... indeed to the regiment as a whole, as the Northumberland Fusiliers, despite its many battalions, had previously earned only two of these medals since the outbreak of the war. Ardent Northumbrians sought to excuse this by alleging that the Fighting Fifth had on some occasion earned the displeasure of Queen Victoria and was thenceforth disqualified from receiving her most coveted award. Whatever truth there may have been in this, the explanation is interesting as the sort of myth that passed among us.'

Gladden, in full prim, and even envy mode, adds an interesting coda, for which there is incidentally no other record to substantiate its veracity:[3]

'A tale was told of our harum-scarum hero [a bit harsh in the circumstances] of whose bravery there could have been not the slightest doubt that on one occasion when making his rounds he had found a dug-out converted into a miniature Monte Carlo, and, instead of putting an immediate end to such a grave deviation from army regulations, he had at once entered into the betting himself! This tale may well have been apocryphal but it certainly hit off the character of the man as it was assessed in the ranks. He was a very unorthodox holder of His Majesty's commission.'

Meanwhile 11th Battalion The Sherwood Foresters was on the extreme right of the British sector, south of Asiago. The Battalion was at first driven back and the Austrians penetrated British positions on the San Sisto Ridge. However, under the gallant command of temporary Lieutenant Colonel C.E. Hudson, The Sherwood Foresters repulsed them. The Austrians failed to capitalise on their initial advantage and the British succeeded in restoring their line.

Hudson was a plantation owner in Ceylon before he went to Sandhurst, failing to complete the Officer's Course. Nevertheless, he joined the Sherwood Foresters, his father's old regiment. The Western Front had seen him awarded the MM, DSO with Bar, and the Croix de Guerre before he was duly awarded the VC. Reading his citation, we get some idea of the maelstrom in which both he and Jack Youll were immersed and, despite it all, were able to demonstrate bravery of the highest calibre – both men undoubtedly saving many lives by their actions.

This is the VC citation for Temporary Lieutenant Colonel C.E. Hudson, 11th Battalion The Sherwood Foresters (Nottinghamshire and Derbyshire Regiment):

> 'For most conspicuous bravery and devotion to duty when his battalion was holding the right front sector during an attack on the British front. The shelling had been very heavy on the right, the trench destroyed, and considerable casualties had occurred, and all the officers on the spot were killed or wounded. This enabled the enemy to penetrate our front line. The enemy pushed their advance as far as the support line which was the key to our right flank. The situation demanded immediate action. Lieutenant Colonel Hudson, recognising its gravity, at once collected various headquarter details, such as orderlies, servants, runners, etc., and, together with some Allies, personally led them up the hill. Driving the enemy down the hill towards our front line, he again led a party of about five up the trench, where there were about 200 enemy, in order to attack them from the flank. He then with two men got out of the trench and rushed the position, shouting to the enemy to surrender, some of whom did. He was then severely wounded by a bomb which exploded on his foot. Although in great pain, he gave directions for the counter-attack to be continued, and this was done successfully, about 100 prisoners and six machine-guns being taken. Without doubt the high courage and determination displayed by Lieutenant Colonel Hudson saved a serious situation, and had it not been for his quick determination in organising the counterattack a large number of the enemy would have dribbled through, and counter-attack on a larger scale would have been necessary to restore the situation.'

Nearly 450 Commonwealth casualties of the Battle of the Piave River are commemorated in Italy by Commonwealth War Graves.[4]

These First World War servicemen are primarily commemorated in four cemeteries and memorials:

- Magnaboschi British Cemetery – Approximately 125 casualties
- Boscon British Cemetery – Approximately 95 casualties
- Granezza British Cemetery – Approximately 60 casualties
- Giavera Memorial – 15 casualties

Chapter 10

The Hero Returns to Thornley, 10 September 1918

Local man wins the Victoria Cross – our premier decoration for valour in the face of the enemy – was huge news in the mining village of Thornley, in County Durham, and in England generally. So, on Tuesday 10 September 1918 at the Thornley Hippodrome, Jack was publicly honoured in recognition of having gained the Victoria Cross. This came in the form of gifts: a gold watch and chain with blue numerals and monogram initials JSY and a large silver initialled cigarette case. He was received with rousing cheers and was characteristically modest and generous in his reply:

> 'There are two kinds of honour, the seen and the unseen. I hope the people of Thornley give the rest of the boys the same recognition on their return.'

Local school children then launched into 'Blighty' and 'The Village Blacksmith'.

The Thornley Soldiers' and Sailors' Memorial and Welcome Home Committee had been set up some time before and had decided to instigate a door-to-door collection for the gifts and for a Memorial. J.B. Foster of the Weardale Coal Company presided while J.E. Rogerson, Chairman, presented the gifts. Mr D. Hagen, Jack's old headmaster, spoke with pride to have been associated with him.[1]

A press report from the time tells us that:

'A few days ago a lad of the new VCs Platoon came home on leave, bringing with him the Italian Silver Medal which had been presented to 2nd Lt Youll by the King of Italy in person. "He is one of the lads. And if anybody ever deserved the VC it is 2nd Lieutenant Youll."'[2]

This is how *The Sunderland Daily Echo & Shipping Gazette* – Monday 19 August 1918 – reported the thanksgiving service:[3]

'THORNLEY VC's RETURN. A special service of thanksgiving was held in Thornley Parish Church yesterday for the safe return to his people and to his native place of Second-Lieut. John Scott Youll, the Thornley VC. There was a large attendance including members of the Thornley Parish Council and other public bodies. These bodies formed up in procession at the bottom of Hartlepool Street, and, headed by the banner of Thornley Miners' Lodge and the Wheatley Hill brass band, paraded to church. Second-Lieut. Youll VC, who is at home on leave, attended the service with his father (Mr. R.W. Youll), his brother (Mr T.W. Youll) and his sisters (Mrs R. Tully and Miss M. Youll) and other relations. The service was preached by the Rev. Godfrey Evans of Castle Eden.'

To say that Jack was a brave soldier is something of an understatement. The award of a VC at the Battle of Asiago apart, we have seen how Jack was also mentioned in despatches in hellish fighting at Polygon Wood near Ypres on 30 May 1914 and was then recommended for a Military Cross for administering to wounded men during a murderous six-hour artillery barrage. This could have occurred either in France or Italy.

Jack's bravery was celebrated in the 26 July issue of the *Illustrated Chronicle*, a Newcastle paper dedicated to publishing information about and photographs of soldiers sent in by relatives and friends. It continues its superb work today by 'scanning their images to make them available online for those tracing family history or anyone with an interest in the First World War'.[4]

Medaglia d'Argento al Valor Militare

As mentioned, he was also recognised by the Italian Secretary of State for War with the highly prestigious award of the Italian Silver Medal of Military Valour and Star (Medaglia d'Argento al Valor Militare), awarded at a ceremony by the King of Italy, Victor Emmanuel III, gazetted 29 November 1918.

Here is the citation:

> 'During a whole day of fighting he was constantly displaying valour. As Patrol Commander, surprised by the enemy's barrage fire, he sent his men to safety and remained alone in observation. During the enemy attack he took command of men from various units, participating in the counter attacks, assaulted an enemy Machine Gun, killed the machine gun team and turned the Gun against the enemy's advancing waves – Asiago 15 June 1918.'

During the First World War, the medal was awarded to military personnel, units above company level and to civilians for outstanding bravery in the face of the enemy. During the war the silver medal was awarded some 38,614 times for individual acts of valour (368 gold medals and 60,244 bronze medals were also awarded).[5] So, this makes the Italian Silver Medal for Military Valour equivalent in frequency and prestige to the British Military Cross, which was awarded some 40,253 times during the First World War. Other recipients of the Medal for Military Valour include Ernest Hemingway and Erwin Rommel.

On 30 July Second Lieutenant J.S. Youll VC was presented with a VC medal ribbon by Major General Sir J.M. Babington, KCMG, CB, in a full strength battalion parade which included two additional companies from the Durham Light Infantry.

Chapter 11

Ernest Hemingway and Edward Brittain in Asiago

Writers, be they novelists, poets, journalists or diarists, can be useful when the histories of a given place are recorded. Writers add a fresh perspective to the archives, records, and official papers that usually form the bedrock of historical reports and the official facts, statistics and numbers. They, like eye witness reports, add a human dimension that amplifies and embellishes the bare, often faceless facts for us. In this case they can be testament to conditions, emotions and experiences that Jack Youll and his comrades would themselves have seen and felt. In particular, Hemingway's description of the bloody carnage that awaited him in the exploded munitions factory surely holds a mirror to the carnage experienced by soldiers on a regular basis during the First World War.

On a purely personal level, Reynolds explains in his *The Young Hemingway* (1998) that when the fledgling writer returned home for recuperation after the First World War; 'Hemingway could not really tell his parents what he thought when he saw his bloody knee'. He was not able to tell them how scared he had been, 'in another country with surgeons who could not tell him in English if his leg was coming off or not'. This is the fear that countless casualties of the Great War must have felt in the field hospitals of Italy, France and Belgium, a fear that we can identify with all the more acutely thanks to Hemingway, who brings a human experience to the endless impersonal and stark casualty figures we read about. Reading Hemingway and Brittain we become privy to situations and scenarios that combatants in any war might recognise.

And so we are lucky to have the words of novelist and poet Ernest Hemingway and of Edward Brittain, brother of VAD nurse Vera Brittain author of *Testament of Youth* and other books which chart her experiences in the First World War.

Ernest Hemingway (1899–1961)

With the USA's entry into the First World War, Hemingway tried to enlist in the US Army, a desire he expressed in several letters to his sister Marcelline, but he failed the physical examination due to defective eyesight. Not to be deterred, Hemingway signed up with the American Red Cross Motor Corps as an ambulance driver.

When he left the US, Hemingway went first to an under-bombardment Paris and Bordeaux, and then received orders to report to a unit in Milan in July 1918. Here an assignment turned up very soon when he was despatched to a bombed munitions factory to collect 'the fragments' of female workers: 'I remember that after we searched quite thoroughly for the complete dead we collected fragments'. A horrific scene he vividly described years later in a short story, *The Natural History of the Dead*, which is Chapter 12 in his *Death in the Afternoon*. Steve Paul provides more detail:

> 'An unexpected assignment turned up immediately. Hemingway and others were sent to the gruesome site of a munitions plant explosion a dozen miles outside Milan. Bodies and body parts were strewn everywhere. "We carried them in like at the General Hospital, Kansas City [which Hemingway knew as a cub reporter on the Kansas Star pre-war]", the young man reported on a postcard he sent back to his former colleagues at *The Star*.'[1]

The carnage Hemingway witnessed here informed his descriptive writing in *A Farewell to Arms* and *Death in the Afternoon* – the carnage has its mirror equivalent in the battlefield carnage that Jack Youll regularly witnessed.

Soon afterwards, Hemingway moved to the town of Schio about 150 miles northeast of Milan in the shadow of the Dolomites where he was employed driving ambulances. Simon Jones sets the scene for Hemingway's connection with the region around the Asiago Plain.[2]

Of course, Rommel cut his teeth in the Valdobbiadene area. Hemingway was an ambulance cyclist, fell in love there and wrote many of his works there. That was along the River Piave, where the US Army was based in the last few months of the war. The victory of 24 October 1918 was largely due to the British success on Papadopoli in the Piave, supplied by the Italian boatmen. They cut through the Austrian lines far exceeding their expected objective, thus allowing the Italian 10th to march on to Vittorio Veneto as it is now called.

'Arsiero, Asiago …'

> 'Arsiero, Asiago,
> Half a hundred more,
> Little border villages,
> Back before the war,
> Monte Grappa, Monte Corno,
> Twice a dozen such,
> In the piping times of peace
> Didn't come to much'[3]

Allpoetry.com analyses this poem, written in Paris in 1922, as follows:

> 'The poem 'Arsiero, Asiago …' reminisces about small Italian border villages that were insignificant before the First World War. The simplicity of the language and the repetition of place names create a sense of familiarity and a nostalgic tone. This poem differs from Hemingway's earlier works, such as 'Hills Like White Elephants', which explore themes of loss and emotional turmoil through complex imagery and symbolism. Instead, 'Arsiero, Asiago …' reflects the

disillusionment and anti-war sentiments prevalent during and after the First World War. It aligns with the modernist movement's focus on fragmentation and the futility of war, reflecting the period's disillusionment with pre-war idealism.'[4]

And then there is the chilling post mortem ghostly reminiscences of *Killed Piave July 8 1918* composed in Chicago in 1921:

Killed Piave July 8 1918

>'Desire and
>All the sweet pulsing aches
>And gentle hurtings
>That were you,
>Are gone into the sullen dark.
>Now in the night you come unsmiling
>To lie with me
>A dull, cold, rigid bayonet
>On my hot-swollen, throbbing soul'[5]

And then there is *A Farewell to Arms* inspired by his 1918 experiences on the Italian front, especially the wound he suffered at Fossalta during the 'Battle of the Solstice' and his subsequent hospitalization in Milan which ignited his passion for American nurse Agnes von Kurowsky.[6]

Sandra Spanier remarks that Hemingway's letters clearly demonstrate how little he saw of or experienced actual conflict, and how he was inclined to romanticise and embellish his wartime exploits. We can also be sure that Hemingway enjoyed:

'Nothing better than sitting in a bar and soaking up war stories. One such encounter with George Macauley Trevelyan (who led a British Red Cross ambulance unit on the Austro-Italian Isonzo Front) provided Hemingway with the genesis for his *A Farwell to Arms* novel, in which the author made liberal use of Trevelyan's accounts of the attack at Piava and the rout of the Italian army in the aftermath of Caporetto ... Hemingway, on the other hand, only arrived in Italy with the American Red Cross in June 1918, so he wouldn't have had any first-hand experience of many of the things vividly written about in *A Farewell to Arms*.'[7]

Hemingway or Trevelyan or a bit of both – we certainly get a good picture of what Jack Youll was experiencing.

In June 1918 Hemingway was dispatched to the Italian Front, at about the same time as Austro-Hungarian troops launched an attack on the Italian army near Lake Maggiore. However, things were somewhat quiet in the area where Hemingway was assigned to work driving his ambulances. He tried to liven up his days and so volunteered for the mobile canteen service that dispensed drinks, cigarettes, post cards and chocolate to soldiers entrenched along the front line. He was then transferred to the canteen between Fornaci, Bassano del Grappa and Fossalta di Piave, villages by the Piave River. He wrote to his mother in a letter that year, that the change gave him more wartime experience: 'I have glimpsed the making of large gobs of history during the Great Battle of the Piave and have been all along the Front from the mountains to the Sea'.

Hemingway had been cycling around there for six days when on the evening of 8 July an Austrian *Minenwerfer* mortar shell exploded very close to him spraying out shrapnel and knocking him unconscious. Hemingway later said of the incident: 'When you go to war as a boy you have a great illusion of immortality. Other people get killed; not you ... Then when you are badly wounded the first time you lose that illusion and you know it can happen to you'. Apparently 227 shards of metal peppered his flesh. It seems that he was hit by machine gun fire as well, and did his utmost to ensure the safety of his fellow Red Cross workers, getting them out of harm's way. The Italian government later awarded him the Silver Medal of Military Valour for his selfless heroism. Rob Ruggenberg describes it all in his *Hemingway's Early Encounters with Death*:

'Later, in a letter, Hemingway wrote: "There was one of those big noises you sometimes hear at the front. I died then. I felt my soul or something coming right out of my body, like you'd pull a silk handkerchief out of a pocket by one corner. It flew all around and then came back and went in again and I wasn't dead any more."

'He crumpled up and two Italian stretcher bearers started over the parapet with him, knowing that he needed swift attention. Austrian machine gunners spotted the party and the three went down under a storm of machine gun bullets, one of which got Hemingway in the shoulder and another ripped through his right knee.

'According to Hemingway one Italian was killed instantly, while the other stretcher bearer had both his legs blown off. A third Italian, who had been standing a few feet away, was badly wounded and this one Ernest, after he had regained consciousness, picked up on his back and carried to the first aid dugout. He later wrote he did not remember how he got there, nor that he carried the man, until the next day, when an Italian officer told him all about it and said that it had been voted to give him a valour medal for the act [the Italian Silver Croce al Merito di Guerra].'

https://greatwar.nl/frames/default-hemingway.html

Evidence for the concussed Hemingway's Lazarus-like acts of bravery after the explosion comes with the Italian citation that accompanied his medal:

'Gravely wounded by numerous pieces of shrapnel from an enemy shell, with an admirable spirit of brotherhood, before taking care of himself, he rendered generous assistance to the Italian soldiers more seriously wounded by the same explosion and did not allow himself to be carried elsewhere until after they had been evacuated.'

He was taken to a nearby field hospital and spent five days there being treated for injuries to his knee and leg before being transferred to the

American Red Cross Hospital at 10 Via Alessandro Manzoni, Milan. It was here he met nurse Agnes von Kurowsky:

> 'Who stole the young Hemingway's heart. She was 7 years his senior and probably wasn't under any illusions as to the true nature of their relationship (granted she showed tenderness towards him, and they spent time together visiting the sites in Milan and drinking Campari's, but there is no evidence that they were ever lovers). That said, he (at least) believed they would both return to the States and be married – but not long after, she transferred to Treviso and thereafter to Torro di Mosto (near Venice) from where she wrote a letter asking Hemingway not to contact her any more because she was engaged to be married to an Italian [major and] noble (although no such marriage ever transpired). Hemingway was heart-broken!'[8]

Ruggenberg quotes the killer blow in Hemingway's January 1919 'dear Ernest' letter:

> 'Agnes even promised to follow Hemingway to America and marry him. Instead, after a while she fell in love with an Italian major, a Neapolitan duke, and broke off the relationship with a "Dear Ernest" letter, letting him know that "I am now & always will be too old & I can't get away from that fact that you're just a boy – a kid. I expect to be married soon. And I hope & pray that after you have thought things out, you'll be able to forgive me & start a wonderful career & show what a man you really are."
>
> 'Six months later, in June 1919, Agnes wrote him again and told him that the Duke's mother had refused to permit his marriage to an 'American adventuress,' and hinted that she wished to renew the romance, but Hemingway did not reply. In 1921 he married Hadley Richardson from St. Louis, who was eight years older than he (Agnes attended to his wedding).'

A Farewell to Arms is of course a fictional story written ten years later, but given Hemingway's meagre first-hand war experience it seems improbable that he would have be able to write so vividly about Caporetto and his ambulance driver's flight therefrom without having first read Trevelyan's factual account in *Scenes from Italy's War*, published in 1919, as research material for his novel – Chapter VII in particular simply has too much in common with *A Farewell to Arms* for it to be purely coincidental.

One aspect of Hemingway's time around the Piave that was probably neither embellished for the novel nor second hand, as it were, is his descriptions of the Italian scenery he could see all around him from his house in a village 'that looked across the river and the plain to the mountains'. At the opening of *A Farewell to Arms* Hemingway tells his readers about the late summer landscape and weather: 'the plain was rich with crops; there were many fruit trees and beyond the plain the mountains were brown and bare … the vineyards were thin and bare-branched too and all the country wet and brown and dead with autumn'. There is no reason to suppose that Jack Youll would not have observed the same when he first arrived on the Italian front.

Hemingway was very lucky: when that Austrian trench mortar round landed, an Italian soldier was standing between the explosion and Hemingway. His name was Fedele Temperini, of 69th Infantry Regiment, Infantry Brigade Ancona, born in Siena, died on 8 July 1918 on the Piave and inadvertently saved Hemingway's life.[9] The same round took off both the legs of a second Italian, and badly wounded a third. It was the latter who was carried to the first aid dug-out by Hemingway.

Hemingway was in hospital for months and had operations on his knee and foot, followed by a further spell of convalescence. He left hospital on 28 October 1918 to continue his work for the Red Cross during the Battle of Vittorio Veneto, however he was back in hospital again on 1 November with jaundice. He was still hospitalised when the war ended a few days later.[10]

The identity of that unfortunate Italian soldier, the accidental hero who shielded Hemingway, has been unknown until 2019, seemingly with little or no effort expended by the author, his publishers or by Hemingway biographers and scholars to research and establish this important detail. Given the great efforts which organisations like the Commonwealth Graves Commission expend on identifying unknown soldiers or warriors, and the very existence of cenotaphs and tombs of the unknown soldier around the world, this is somewhat disappointing, and sad – surely it is a case of cold negligence to allow it to remain a cold case for so long?

However, *The Washington Post* in a review of *The Ambulance Drivers: Hemingway, Dos Passos, and a Friendship Made and Lost in War* by James McGrath Morris finally gives us, with the help of historian Marino Perissinotto, the identity of that human shield: it is Fedele Temperini of Montalcino, a medieval city in Tuscany. He was 26 years old the day he died for literature and paved the way for Hemingway's classic books.[11]

On the banks of the Piave River there is a memorial near the spot of the explosion. 'On this levee', the inscription reads in Italian, 'Ernest Hemingway, American Red Cross volunteer, was wounded the night of July 8, 1918'. No mention of Fedele Temperini or his comrades.

Hemingway's experiences around Asiago also inspired three short stories featuring the fictional Nick Adams, who is often considered Hemingway's alter-ego – 'Now I Lay Me', 'In Another Country' and 'A Way You'll Never Be'.

Edward Brittain MC (30 November 1895 – 15 June 1918)

Edward Brittain, like Hemingway, had no direct connection with Jack Youll other than that all three saw action (Hemingway as an ambulance driver, of course) on the Italian Front, on the Asagio Plain and along the banks of the Piave River. However, the experiences recounted by Hemingway and by Vera Brittain on behalf of her brother give us their shared experiences and a clearer picture of the conflict and combat that all three will have experienced.

When Vera Brittain's brother Edward was killed in Italy in June 1918, it was the last in a series of tragedies which cruelly punctuate Vera Brittain's memoir *Testament of Youth*, describing her experience as a VAD nurse in France and Malta. She had already lost her fiancé, Roland Leighton, to a sniper's bullet just before Christmas, 1915. Another close friend, Geoffrey Thurlow, was killed in action in April, 1917. Brittain was one of the first female students to be granted leave by her college, Somerville, to assist in the war effort.

Edward Brittain had applied for a temporary commission in September 1914 and was duly commissioned as a temporary second lieutenant into the Sherwood Foresters (Nottinghamshire and Derbyshire Regiment) on 19 November 1914 when he was still not yet nineteen years of age. He eventually joined the 11th Sherwood Foresters in February 1916, whereupon he was seriously wounded in the left arm and the right thigh at the Battle of the Somme on 1 July 1916. Lieutenant Brittain was evacuated to First London General Hospital, where his sister was a VAD nurse. He was later awarded the Military Cross for his bravery on the Somme. The citation stated that Brittain was awarded the MC 'For conspicuous gallantry and leadership during an attack. He was severely wounded, but continued to lead his men with great bravery and coolness until a second wound disabled him'.[12]

Brittain stayed in England, recuperating until 30 June 1917, his return to active service repeatedly delayed, apparently, by his CO who took a dim view of Edward's supercilious attitude. Geoffrey Thurlow, a fellow officer whom he befriended, was killed in action at Monchy-le-Preux in April 1917; Victor Richardson, a close friend from Uppingham School, was blinded at Arras soon after, and died from a cerebral abscess in London in June 1917.

These losses changed Brittain, in his sister's words, into 'an unfamiliar, frightening Edward, who never smiled or spoke except about trivial things …Silent, uncommunicative, thrust in upon himself'.[13] Edward Brittain eventually returned to the Western Front a year or so after he had left it and was immediately plunged into battle, quite unfamiliar both with the terrain and the men he was commanding. His letters home became increasingly critical of how the war was being prosecuted. Vera Brittain was posted to a British hospital in northern France in August 1917, but she never managed to see her brother there.

Brittain was made up to a temporary captain in August 1917 and was posted to the Italian Front with the 11th Sherwood Foresters in November 1917.[14] He saw his family for the last time on leave in January 1918.

This all coincided on 15 June 1918 when the Austro-Hungarian army launched a major offensive in Italy, part of which was directed at British forces on the Asiago plateau. The 11th Sherwood Foresters were holding San Sisto Ridge, a small but steep wooded hill 60 metres above the plain. Two companies of the Sherwood Foresters held the front line in front of the ridge, just within the tree line. Captain Brittain commanded 'A' Company, holding the right hand section of the front line.

In front were pickets of about ten men from each company armed with four machine guns. At 3.00 am the Austrians opened up and bombarded the British positions: this went on for four hours and was made all the more deadly by the gas shells that were coming over. So great were the toxic chemicals that the waves of gas rolled down the rear slope of San Sisto Ridge into the valley behind. At 6.45 am things got worse for the British when enemy troops led by small groups of stormtroopers armed with flamethrowers began emerging through gaps in the Austrian wire.

While all of this was going on Edward Brittain was liaising with French troops immediately to his right. After the bombardment had taken its toll, his Company had about 50 men left to hold about 800 yards of front line; it is likely that he was the only officer in the Company who was not wounded. One of the Company's two machine guns was shot up but the picket responded, along with the remaining machine gun which spat out 1,000 rounds and inflicted heavy losses on the attackers.

However, the attackers succeeded in outflanking the picket and machine gun, forcing them to withdraw, enabling the Austrians to crawl towards the British wire and find a route through at the junction of the two Sherwood companies. Having penetrated the British trenches, the stormtroopers were followed by trench clearing parties methodically working their way through left and right with grenades and flamethrowers, capturing 200 yards of the British front line.

In the words of the 23rd Division GS War Diary,[14] 'the 11th Sherwoods were holding the front line with D Company on the left and Brittain's A Company on the right; C Company was on the ridge summit behind. Machine guns R1 and R2 were deployed in front of the British wire, as was a picquet of ten men.'

It was not long before up to 200 Austrians were crawling all over the British trench, as the Sherwoods valiantly attempted to block the trench at either end of the intrusion.

Brittain immediately counterattacked, pushing some of the Austrians back through the wire, and reorganised his defence. It was when he was doing this that he was killed, shot through the head by a sniper.

Simon Jones tells us how:

'Brittain's Company was now operating without any officers while the Austrians could boast at least ten machine guns now installed inside the British wire. They kept on pouring through the gap filling the British front line: about thirty enemy pushed up a communication trench to the summit of the ridge into an undefended length of trench.

'A counterattack organised by the commanding officer of the 11th Sherwood Foresters, a 26-year-old Lieutenant Colonel, Charles Hudson, forced the Austrians back and retook the ridge but soon afterwards Hudson was seriously wounded by a grenade. A second British counterattack consolidated the hold on the front line.'[15]

Edward Brittain is buried in Granezza British Cemetery on the Asiago Plateau.[16] In September 1921 Vera Brittain visited the cemetery with her close friend and fellow feminist Winifred Holtby, and her will requested that her ashes be scattered on his grave: 'for nearly 50 years much of my heart has been in that Italian village cemetery'. Her daughter, Shirley Williams, honoured her request in September 1970.

Bravery, patriotism, selflessness and honour – these are all qualities that Edward Brittain demonstrated in his short life, and they are virtues for which he is remembered and rightly so.

Nevertheless, much attention has also been paid to Edward's homosexuality and his activities at Uppingham School as revealed to his sister by their mother. The allegations were substantiated by Edward's CO who suspected Edward's homosexuality and, defying orders from above, warned him that he would be court-martialled when he returned from the line. Hence the belief grew that Edward deliberately put himself in the firing line to avoid the shame that would rebound on his family and regiment should his sexual preferences be revealed.

The incident says more about the values – and hypocrisy – of the day than anything else, not least Brittain's valour, patriotism, selflessness and honour. Heroism does not discriminate when it comes to sexual orientation.

Chapter 12

Jack Youll Killed in Action at the Battle of Vittorio Veneto, October 1918

Despite its immense importance and significance in the annals of the First World War, the decisive Battle of Vittorio Veneto, (24 Oct–4 Nov 1918), a pivotal Italian victory and the final offensive launched on the Italian Front during the First World War, is comparatively little known, even neglected in twentieth-century political and military history. The battle led to what can only be described as the implosion of the once mighty multinational Hapsburg Empire. The destruction of the Austro-Hungarian army dramatically and irrevocably redrew the political map of central Europe. In short the Italian victory marked the end of the war on the Italian Front, secured the dissolution of the Austro-Hungarian Empire and contributed to the end of the First World War just one week later. Erich Ludendorff (1865–1937) says of it:

> 'In Vittorio Veneto, Austria did not lose a battle, but lost the war and itself, dragging Germany in its fall. Without the destructive battle of Vittorio Veneto, we would have been able, in a military union with the Austro-Hungarian monarchy, to continue the desperate resistance through the whole winter, in order to obtain a less harsh peace, because the Allies were very fatigued.'[1]

Under political pressure to act before the Austro-Hungarians secured armistice arrangements with US President Woodrow Wilson, Italian commander-in-chief General Armando Diaz launched a major offensive across the Piave River and north against the strongpoint of Monte Grappa. Diaz was determined to act only when he believed Italy would strike with success guaranteed. In his offensive, three of the five armies lining the front from the Monte Grappa sector to the Adriatic end of the Piave were to drive across the river towards Vittorio Veneto, so as to cut communications between the two Austrian armies opposing them. With the Piave in flood, Diaz first attacked Monte Grappa on 24 October. Nevertheless, there was little to show after three days of heavy fighting against an intractable defence.

To make matters much worse, on 1 November, the new Hungarian government of Count Mihály Károlyi decided to recall all of the troops who were conscripted from the territory of the Kingdom of Hungary – a massive blow for the Habsburgs' armies.

The battle led to the capture of over 5,000 artillery pieces and over 350,000 Austro-Hungarian troops, including 120,000 Germans, 83,000 Czechs and Slovaks, 60,000 South Slavs, 40,000 Poles, several tens of thousands of Romanians and Ukrainians, and 7,000 Austro-Hungarian loyalist Italians and Friulians.[2]

Allied forces totalled 57 infantry divisions, including 52 Italian, three British (23rd, 7th and 48th under the command of Earl Cavan), two French (23rd and 24th),[3] and the 332nd US Infantry Regiment, along with supporting arms. The Austro-Hungarian army had 46 infantry divisions and six cavalry divisions, but both sides were ravaged by influenza and malaria and the Austrians could call on only 6,030 guns to the Allies' 7,700; from 24 to 31 October alone, the Italian artillery fired 2,446,000 shells. The Allies had 600 aircraft (93 Anglo-French, including four RAF squadrons) to give them total air superiority.

Chris Baker takes up the story:[4]

'September 1918

'The 23rd Division was moved from the Asiago Plateau [to relieve the Italian XI Corps' front on the River Piave from Salletuol to Palazzon], and was billeted in an area north-west of Vicenza before moving by rail to Treviso. It was part of a wider movement, with the British Army taking over a wide front on the banks of the

River Piave, downstream from its former positions on the Montello. The Piave here is a mighty river indeed: 800 yards or more wide, very fast-flowing in numerous deep channels. A feature facing the British was a flat, narrow, four-mile-long island – Papadopoli. This move was part of a broad plan by the Italian Commander-in-Chief General Diaz to make a decisive break through across the Piave, to separate the Austrian forces on this front from those in the Trentino. If a major advance could be secured in this area – the Vittorio Veneto[5] – then the enemy's rail routes for supply would be cut and they would be forced to withdraw their troops from Italian soil. The attack commenced in October 1918.'

Baker continues with some detail about the involvement of the 11th Northumberland Fusiliers in the battle, and of course, of Jack Youll:

'On 27 October 1918, the 7th and 23rd Divisions attacked in the Vittorio Veneto. This followed a successful effort by the 7th Division to cross part of the river and capture Papadopoli Island. The 11th Northumberland Fusiliers were the leftmost Battalion in this attack, and their job was to produce a flank defence as the rest of the Divisions forced a crossing of the river. There was a gap of some 5,000 yards to the next formation, the Italian 58th Division. They were to move across right, to converge with the 23rd Division to form a continuous line. This however, failed as the Italians could not cross the river [which was swollen].

'The river crossing was indeed arduous, with men crossing by sections, mostly by linking arms and dragging their feet along the bottom; to have lifted a foot in the incredible current would almost certainly mean losing their footing and being swept away. A few men were washed off their feet and drowned. As the barrage lifted off the bank, the whole line rushed forward. Machine-gun fire was heavy, and amongst others Lieutenant Colonel Ashton St. Hill, the CO of the battalion, was killed. The British bombardment had not destroyed much of the wire, but this was thin in places where the men could trample it down, whilst other gaps were cut by hand under covering fire from Lewis guns. Through these gaps platoons passed and then extended, and the bayonet did the rest. It was reported that no Austrian had his bayonet fixed; many surrendered, others ran. In spite of resistance, in which the 11th Battalion lost all its senior officers so that it was soon led only by a Lieutenant, the whole Bund on the front of the 23rd Division was in its possession.[6] The Battalion was relieved by the 10th later in the morning. It was by now weak through losses, and was reorganised as two Companies.'

The battalion War Diary of the 11th Sherwood Foresters adds more detail:[7]

'On 27 October the left of the Divisional Front from the 68th IB with 12th DLI and 11th NF on right and left respectively met with stiff resistance and uncut wire. Considerable trouble was experienced from machine gun fire from the left flank and from certain forward machine guns which had escaped the barrage. At this point the 11th NF suffered severe casualties, their commanding officer, Lieutenant Colonel St. Hill DSO, being killed. And all officers over the rank of lieutenant becoming casualties. The command of the battalion fell to Lieutenant J. Robertson. Both battalions, however, continued to advance with great gallantry, overcame all resistance and completed the capture of the first objective simultaneously with the 69th Infantry Brigade on their right.'

The Italian 10th Army maintained its ground and established a bridgehead 2.5 miles deep and 5 miles broad. The British captured 3,520 prisoners and 54 guns. Svetozar Boroević von Bojna, the Austro-Hungarian commander, ordered a counter-attack on the Italian bridgeheads on the same day, but his troops mutinied – a serious problem the Austrians would have to face from then on – and the counter-attack failed.

Jack Youll Killed in Action at the Battle of Vittorio Veneto

Jack Youll Killed in Action

Tragically, on 27 October 1918, Jack Youll was one of sixty comrades killed during the attack across the River Piave. In the attack the Division had three objectives in its sights. The first was taken with all officers wounded except Youll. At the capture of the second objective, Youll was wounded in the arm, but the wound was only slight. The Army Chaplain arrived and advised him to stay where he was, as the passage of the river was being heavily shelled. About 6 pm, the Chaplain returned to the bridge and found Youll's body laid out on a stretcher. He had been struck by a shell. His last words had been; 'It's all right Cowling (his adjutant), we got them stone cold'.

This is how Norman Gladden sensitively and respectfully describes what came to be Jack Youll's last hours:

'After this short delay we pushed forward quickly and at the edge of an extensive ploughed field came up with an officer and an NCO of another company, who were collecting stragglers before advancing across to the far hedge, which seemed a likely hide-out for the defence. We strung out in open order and continued our progress, expecting at any moment to hear the rattle of a machine gun ahead, but still nothing untoward happened. Coming in from the right – it was a characteristic of our flank position that everything came from the right that morning – we saw an officer approaching who, as he came nearer, we recognised as the battalion's VC; he had been wounded in the hand and was going back to the rear to have it dressed. We waved and wished him the best of luck, not without the usual streak of jealousy for his good fortune. Later I heard that he had been killed crossing one of the pontoons, which was receiving attention from the Austrian artillery. Such is the futility of military glory. A brave man dies by a chance shell as easily as a coward. Neither bravery nor cowardice are keys to survival in the days of high explosive.'

The Battalion War Diary alarmingly reported on 27 October that all officers had become casualties, including Youll killed in action. The Battalion was then reorganised into two companies. Norman Gladden writes in his *Across the Piave* that Youll had been wounded in the hand and was returning to a dressing station when he was killed by an Austrian shell while crossing a pontoon bridge.

The narrative later used in the Spink *Prospectus* for the sale of Jack's medals is a close version of this:

> 'His Adjutant, Lieutenant Cowling, afterwards was ordered to attack, with three objectives to take. On the taking of the first objective all the Officers of Youll's Company, with the exception of Youll himself, became casualties. At the capture of the second objective, Youll was wounded in the arm, but the wound was only slight. About noon, he was seen by Chaplain Wells in a captured trench and the pair had some lunch together. The Chaplain advised the young officer to stay where he was, as the passage of the river was being heavily shelled. About 6 pm, the Chaplain returned to the bridge and there was Youll's body laid out on a stretcher. He had been struck by a shell. His last words were "It's all right Cowling, we got them stone cold".'

There is in the archives of the Regimental Museum of the Northumberland Fusiliers a framed photograph of Jack; on the back there is an extract from Rupert Brooke's *The Dead*, along with a hand written epitaph written in ink below:

> 'Blow out, you bugles, over the rich Dead!
> There's none of these so lonely and poor of old,
> But, dying, has made us rarer gifts than gold.
> These laid the world away; poured out the red
> Sweet wine of youth; gave up the years to be
> Of work and joy, and that unhoped serene,

> That men call age; and those who would have been,
> Their sons, they gave, their immortality.
> 			Lt. Jack Youll VC of Thornley Co. Durham.
> 			Killed in Italy 1918, in his 21st year.'

The tributes started to come very soon after reports of Jack Youll's death. *The St George's Gazette*, the regimental magazine, was quick to run an obituary.[8]

It was later noted that at 6.45 am on 27 October, the attack captured all objectives in spite of strong resistance and counter attacks on Borgo Melanotte. During the day the Division had captured 2,200 prisoners. A week later the Armistice came into effect and the shooting and shelling stopped.

Victory at Vittorio Veneto and an Armistice

On 29 October, the Italian Eighth Army pushed on towards Vittorio Veneto, its advance guard of lancers and *Bersaglieri* cyclists entered on the morning of 30 October. The Italian Third Army forced a crossing of the lower Piave, while raids in the mountains disclosed that the Austrians were withdrawing there. Reserves, including the 332nd US Infantry Regiment streamed over the Piave behind the Italian Tenth Army.

Vittorio Veneto was taken the following day by the Italian Eighth Army, which was already pushing on to the Tagliamento River. Trieste was taken by an amphibious expedition on 3 November. The Italian Eighth Army troops which had managed to cross the Piave were only able to communicate with the west bank by using swimmers. The swimmers were supported by the elite assault Arditi Corps, the *Caimani del Piave* ('Caimans of the Piave'). Eighty-two had been recruited by Captain Remo Pontecorvo Bacci after the catastrophic Battle of Caporetto. Armed with a *resolza* knife and two hand grenades, they put their training to the test when they remained in the torrential currents of the icy Piave for up to sixteen hours; fifty died in the river during the campaign, a casualty rate of over 60 per cent.⁹ The Italian Twelfth Army, commanded by French General Jean Graziani, continued to advance, supported on the right by the Eighth Army.

At dawn on 31 October, the Italian Fourth Army resumed the offensive on Monte Grappa and this time was able to advance beyond the old Austrian positions towards Feltre. In the mountains and on the plain, the Allied armies pushed on until an armistice was arranged. Austria-Hungary lost about 30,000 killed and wounded and 300,000 prisoners (50,000 by 31 October; 100,000 by 1 November; 300,000 by 4 November). The Italians captured 448,000 Austrian-Hungarian soldiers (about one-third of the Imperial-Royal Army), 24 of whom were generals, 5,600 cannon and mortars, and 4,000 machine guns.

During the 10 days' struggle the Italians suffered 37,461 casualties (dead and wounded) – 24,507 of them on Monte Grappa. British casualties were 2,139, while the French lost 778 men.

The Armistice of Villa Giusti was signed on 3 November at 15.20, to become effective 24 hours later, at 15.00 on 4 November.

On October 29, the attack had advanced the front towards the next river crossing: the Monticano. The Battalion crossed this river successfully and moved ahead, with its right on the little River Cervada. There was considerable resistance from machine-guns hidden in houses and ditches, but the attack was completely successful and by 6.30 pm the 11th had cleared the enemy from the whole Brigade front.

The assault across the Piave was a great success; as well as the great advance made, some 300,000 prisoners were taken; more, in fact, than the entire Allied force attacking on this front. This was in addition to an enormous amount of booty comprising much materiel. The 7th and 23rd Divisions had played a prominent part, for the loss of just under 1,600 men of the average 78,000 deployed between 27 October and 4 November. Reductions of the British force in Italy were gradually carried out, with the very last returning home on 15 April 1920.¹⁰

To heighten the tragedy yet further, Jack Youll, still only twenty-one, had died just a fortnight before Armistice Day. His parents were notified

Jack Youll Killed in Action at the Battle of Vittorio Veneto

of his death in a telegram sent on 10 November, just one day before the fighting stopped.

Just as poignant was the cruel fact (with equally cruel timing) that it was reported in the *Newcastle Journal* (29 November 1918) that a Thornley Peace Celebration Committee had been set up.

In an article headed *'Northumberlands in Italy: Situation Saved by Valour'* the Italian High Command approved of what was 'a well-deserved tribute to the splendid valour of men of a regiment with glorious traditions'.

Youll was initially buried at Lonadina British Cemetery, Spresiano, but in June 1919 he was later reburied at Giavera British Cemetery.

In 1997, his medal group including the VC, British War Medal 1914–20, Victory Medal 1914–19 and Italian Silver Star were sold at Spink for £36,000. They were purchased by the Ashcroft Trust and displayed in the Ashcroft Gallery, Imperial War Museum.

Giavera British Cemetery is the last resting place of 415 British casualties, as well as Jack Youll. His grave can be found at Giavera British Cemetery, Arcade Plot 1. Row H. Grave 2.[11]

Lance Corporal Francis Crawshaw Raynes (1895–1918): Another 11th Battalion Vittorio Veneto Fatality

Much like the writers referred to above, the experiences of other combatants in the same or entirely different combat zones can shed useful light on what Jack Youll was up against and the kind of thing he was experiencing on a daily basis on the Western and Italian Fronts.

The very same day in the very same operation Jack Youll was killed, 285138 Lance Corporal Francis Crawshaw Raynes died at the Battle of Vittorio Veneto, age 23. Like Jack Youll his unit was the 11th Northumberland Fusiliers. He was the son of Stephen Henry and Hannah Elizabeth Raynes of Sheffield. Francis is buried in Tezze British Cemetery (Plot 5. Row C. Grave 10) and like Jack Youll died a week before the Austrian army signed the Armistice on November 4 1918.[12]

The village of Tezze was captured by the Austrians in the advance in the autumn of 1917 and remained in their hands until the Allied forces crossed the River Piave at the end of October 1918. The Allied attack east of the Piave began early in the morning of 27 October. Despite stiff resistance and difficulties with bringing forward supporting troops across the river, the Austrians were forced back over the next few days until the Armistice came into effect on 4 November. Many of those who died on the north-east side of the river during the passage of the Piave are buried in Tezze British Cemetery. It now contains 356 Commonwealth burials of the First World War, 335 of whom have been identified.[13]

Armistice

Jack Youll was within an ace of surviving the war. His family must have felt cheated, so close was he to coming home. The systematic telegraphic systems which dictated when they were told the shocking news were just that: systematic – and could not take any account of timings or circumstances.

In Italy, it seems that Jack's comrades received the news of the armistice with relief that it was all over and were impatient to get home; there was little or none of the celebrating that was taking place in London and in other large towns and cities.

In Thornley a glimpse of the concert given in the Hippodrome Theatre by Thornley Workmen's Soldiers and Sailors Help Fund shines light on the carnage visited on this small village by the war which was sure to end all wars. Carnage which afflicted most cities, towns, villages and hamlets the length and breadth of the kingdom and which is often a forgotten legacy of all wars:[14]

> 'During the past year they had paid to disabled soldiers and their dependants the sum of £289.19s.2d and to the widows and children of fallen soldiers £226.2s making a total disbursement of £516,1s.2d. They had on the books 38 disabled soldiers, 35 wives of disabled

soldiers, 102 children of disabled soldiers, 40 widows of fallen soldiers and 94 fatherless children. In addition to these amounts they had handed out £70 in the shape of Christmas Boxes.'

Tellingly, Mr Joseph Carey saw this as an indication of true brotherhood and sympathy with those who had fought and suffered in the country's battles:

> 'They must remember that though the war was over those who had suffered through it were still with us, and it was the intention of the committee to continue to appeal to the public for support until the Government had seen its way to make ample provision for those who had been maimed and the dependants of those who had lost their husbands and fathers in the great struggle.'

Meanwhile, in early 1919 demobilisation continued at a rapid pace with around 35,000 men leaving the services every day: one out of every four was retained to populate the new peace army.

Another man who did not live to see mobilization was Mrs Jane Welsh's husband of Hartlepool Street; 38575 Private Matthew Youll (b.1877) who served with the DLI had been missing since March 1918 and was now presumed dead. Private Youll was landlord of the Queen's Head Hotel and a member of Thornley Parish Council.[15] He was eventually buried in Pozieres Memorial CWGC Cemetery/Memorial Somme [Source:7432661].

On 18 July 1919 Jack Youll was remembered at the Thornley Presentation to Local Heroes. A procession was headed by the Thornley Colliery Brass Band ably supported by children from Thornley Council School and St Godric's School, the Salvation Army Band and Thornley Ragtime Band. All told, 'about 1,000 children were regaled with tea and about 200 aged people and soldiers' widows were similarly entertained'.

Balloons were sent up and deck flares obtained from the Admiralty were lit. A bonfire on the American Hill was the high point, but this got a bit out of hand when one of the spectators climbed on top of it. A ladder was swiftly brought and he was dragged down before the flames reached him.[16]

There was soon more bad and sad news for the Youll family, this time relating to the death of Jack's mother and her funeral as reported in *The Hartlepool Northern Daily Mail* of Wednesday 14 November 1923:

> 'Thornley. Funeral of VC's mother. The remains of Mrs. Youll, wife of Mr. Richard Youll, of Thornley, and mother of the late 2nd-Lieut. Jack Youll, N.F., the Thornley VC hero, were laid to rest in Thornley Churchyard Tuesday afternoon in the presence of a deeply sympathetic gathering. The Rev. Hamilton Blackwood (Vicar of Thornley) performed the last sad rites. The hymns, 'Jesu, lover of soul', and 'For ever with the Lord', were sung, and Mr. Albert H. Oswald played 'The Dead March in Saul'. Mrs. Youll had been an invalid for about six years.'

Chapter 13

Lord Ashcroft's Hero of the Month

As noted, Jack Youll's decorations were sold by Spink & Son, medal specialists since 1666, on 17 December 1997.[1] Jack Youll's medals now form part of the Lord Ashcroft collection on display in the Lord Ashcroft Gallery in the Imperial War Museum. Uniquely, they are displayed under one of seven different qualities of bravery. Lord Ashcroft (b. 1946) feels that Temporary Second Lieutenant John Scott Youll's VC medal group falls within the category of skill: 'Wisdom, sound judgement and technical knowledge are the hallmarks of Skill. It is about using resources to greatest effect usually under intense pressure. For many involved in bomb disposal, while a single movement might start the clock ticking, the puzzle still has to be solved, the game won. Perseverance is everything.'

So Jack Youll falls under the 'Skill' category and although he was not a bomb disposal officer he did, in the estimation of Lord Ashcroft, display all the qualities required of that group of heroes.

Lord Ashcroft tells us that:

'Tragically, Youll, still only twenty-one, had died just a fortnight before Armistice Day. His parents were notified of his death in a telegram sent on 10 November, just a single day before the fighting halted. Youll was initially buried at Lonadina British Cemetery, Spresiano, but he was later reburied at Giavera British Cemetery, also in Italy ... I purchased his VC medal group at an auction in London in 1997 and I feel immensely privileged to have become the custodian of this courageous man's gallantry and service awards.'

Chapter 14

Thomas Kenny VC, W. McNally VC and W. Wood VC

Of course, Jack Youll was not the only courageous soldier to have been awarded the VC in the theatres of war where Jack was active. The three other local men described in this chapter demonstrate, each in their own way, how they too attained the pinnacle of courage in the face of the enemy and, in so doing, reflect the valour displayed by Jack Youll and the type of situations in which Jack was to find himself.[1] The three share with Jack either the same regiment, the same battles or are local to Thornley.

Thomas Kenny VC

'All I can say is that I did my duty in France to the best of my ability.'

The Wheatley Hill Heritage Centre website tells us that:[2]

'Thomas Kenny was born at [Front Street] South Wingate [a mining village close to Thornley] otherwise known as Hartbrushes on 4 April 1882. After he left St Mary's Roman Catholic School at Wingate, he worked as a quarryman and later as a miner.'

In 1901 home was Pond Street, South Wingate. He married when he was 21 years of age in 1903. He was married to Isabella Applegarth from Coxhoe at St Peter's and Paul's Roman Catholic Church, Hutton Henry where the Kennys now lived; they had seven children before the First World War. At the time of the 1911 census Thomas, his wife and children were living at Walker's Buildings, Hartbushes. Thomas was the eldest brother of four children, John and two sisters – Annie and Winifred. He and Isabella had a further seven children after the First World War.

Who knows what made Thomas Kenny and thousands like him, in steady employment, leave his family, home and work in 1914 to join the Army. He was not conscripted and the production of coal was more important than ever with the onset of war, but on 16 September 1914 Thomas Kenny was one of the new recruits for 13th DLI and served as Private 17424. Patriotism, a keen sense of duty and an innate bravery must have been high on the list of reasons.

Kenny was assigned to 'B' company on 16 September 1914, one of the new recruits for the 13th DLI who were sent south by train from Newcastle upon Tyne to Bullswater Camp near Pirbright in Surrey to join the 68th Brigade of the 23rd Division. The battalion was also based in Aldershot, Ashford and Bramshott before crossing to France on 25 August 1915.

The task of effective training was made all the more difficult by:

> 'a lack of instructors, experienced officers and non-commissioned officers. Added to this was the shortage of uniforms, rifles and equipment and the dreadful state of the camp at Bullswater. The Battalion lived in tents until the end of November and suffered badly in the rain, mud and cold.'

The website continues:

> 'Private 17424 Thomas Kenny, 'B' Company, 13th (Service) Battalion DLI landed at Boulogne on 26 August 1915, nearly a year after he had volunteered. Training immediately began in France to prepare the men for the trenches and the battalion were asked to provide working parties, probably as a result of the high numbers of miners in their ranks.'

The battalion relieved the 12th (Service) Battalion of the DLI at Bois Grenier near Armentières.

We get a vivid and real life description of the battalion's life in the trenches from the correspondence Lieutenant Philip Anthony Brown sent to his mother. Brown was born in Kent and, after studying at New College, Oxford, in 1911 he moved to Newcastle-upon-Tyne to work as a tutor with the Worker's Educational Association (WEA). The following year he became a lecturer at Durham University:

> 'About 12.30 am a man came and said he could hear moaning over the parapet. I was afraid that this meant that some of my men, who had started on a listening patrol, had been hit ... I went down with my observer, a very nice Irishman from County Durham, who goes with me everywhere, and crept along ... a very shallow trench. We soon came on one man down in the bottom of the ditch. It was difficult to move him but finally my observer got him on his back. Poor fellow had a bad wound in the side.'

And later: on 2 November 1915 at about 18.30 during torrential rain the 13th Battalion DLI relieved the 12th in front line trenches 1.26. 3–5 opposite La Houssoie near Armentieres. He wrote to his mother, in what was to be his last letter home:

> 'We have gone back to the trenches – and to such trenches. I don't think any words can adequately describe them. It has been raining ... there is not a patch of dry ground anywhere. Boards soaked in mud, sandbags bursting with mud, ponds and even wells of mud ... yellow mud, greasy ponds, dirty clothes and heaps of mangled sandbags. A great deal of the trenchwork is collapsing in the wet, as was to be expected, and it keeps us busy reconstructing it ... I am on duty and should go the rounds.'

The observer in question was Thomas Kenny, working his first night on the battalion's first tour of duty. At 9.15 pm on 4 November he accompanied Lieutenant Brown, officer of the watch, on a visit to a party working on barbed wire in front of trench 1.26.4. Dense fog enveloped no-man's land: very soon the two men were hopelessly lost; it was at about 9.45, the website continues, when a

> '... shot rang out and Lieutenant Brown fell, shot through both thighs. Thomas Kenny at once went to his aid and hoisted Lieutenant Brown onto his back. Immediately heavy rifle fire opened up from the German lines, forcing Private Kenny to crawl through the mud, but still he kept his badly wounded officer on his back. Lieutenant Brown begged Kenny to go on alone and leave him but Kenny refused. When bursts of fire were too severe, he lay still, only starting again when the firing slackened. This ordeal lasted for nearly an hour, before Private Kenny, cold, wet and utterly exhausted, at last stumbled upon a ditch he recognised. He made Lieutenant Brown as comfortable as he could and started off to find his battalion's front line.
>
> 'Thomas Kenny arrived at the battalion listening post in Trench 1.26.4 at just after 11 pm and found Captain G. White. After hearing Kenny's story, Captain White asked for volunteers to go with him out to no-man's-land. Two stretcher bearers plus Privates Thomas Kerr and Michael Brough [both from Stanley in Co. Durham] volunteered. Private Kenny, despite his exhaustion, his torn uniform and his bleeding hands and legs, then led them to where he had left his wounded officer.'

All the while the Germans were 30 yards away, firing and lobbing grenades; two of the other volunteers – 16874 Private Robert Watt from West Hartlepool and Private Ernest McClane, from Middlesbrough – were killed, or died from wounds.

When he arrived back at the battalion's trenches, Lieutenant Brown, in spite of his critical wounds and weakening from loss of blood, regained consciousness briefly and was heard to say; 'Well Kenny, you're a hero'. Philip Brown died whilst he was being carried to the dressing station.[3]

Kenny was the first soldier from the Durham Light Infantry to win the VC in the First World War. He was promoted to Company Sergeant Major soon after.[4]

The website reports:

'On 4 March 1916, Lance Sergeant Thomas Kenny was presented with his Victoria Cross by King George V at Buckingham Palace. Mrs Brown, the mother of Philip Brown, was there to meet and thank the man who had tried so hard and for so long to save her son's life. This was to be the start of a long, lasting friendship between the two families.'

Mrs Brown took him to her home in Beckenham, Kent; one of Kenny's daughters went into domestic service with Lieutenant Brown's brother. *The Durham Chronicle & Seaham Weekly News* (3 December 1948) reported that Mrs Brown was there at Buckingham Palace that day. We also know that every year, on the anniversary of his VC action, Thomas Kenny was gifted money from Mrs Brown, and that her daughter continued this after her death, even though she had moved to Canada. The last installment arrived one month or so before Thomas Kenny's death.

Here is the text of a moving letter sent by Mrs Brown to Thomas, from Broomhill, Southend Road, Beckenham:

'I am writing to express to you the deep gratitude I feel to you for your most gallant and heroic service on the 4th November, when you risked your life over and over again in rescuing Lieutenant Brown after he was wounded. I am thankful to feel that he died amongst friends, and that he was able to thank you. I know that you would value his last words. He has often mentioned you in his letters home as 'a very nice Irishman from County Durham, who goes with me everywhere'. I am glad to hear that your heroism will be recognised and rewarded. You have earned our deepest gratitude, and I can never thank you enough. I pray that you may be spared to see the hour of victory, which surely will come.'

It is highly unlikely that any of us will ever receive a letter of such poignancy or depth of emotion, but these are the sensations that war and the camaraderie it fosters uniquely bring out in us.

Major C.E. Walker of the 13th DLI wrote to Mrs Kenny saying how proud the battalion was of her husband for the 'magnificent pluck and endurance he showed under very heavy fire', adding that 'as soon as they rose a rifle was fired from a listening post about 15 yards away. Lieutenant Brown fell, shot through both thighs, and Kenny at once went to his assistance, and, although Lieutenant Brown was a good sized man he got him on his back and started off with him.' The Germans opened rapid fire causing Kenny to drop to his hands and knees, and he began crawling with the officer, and this continued for over an hour. Lieutenant Brown's last words were 'Kenny, you're a hero'.

Mrs Walker, wife of Major Walker, added to the correspondence with a letter from Queen Anne's Gardens, St James's Park, London, saying:

> 'How very glad she was to hear of his brave deed, and tendering her congratulations. If this war had done nothing else, it had shown how brave Englishmen could be. She could imagine no finer act than to risk one's life for a friend.'

Mrs White, wife of Captain White of Stanley Mansions, Park Walk, Fulham Road in London, added her congratulations on the 'brave deed' and how proud 'B' Company was of him; finishing with her sorrow at Lieutenant Brown's death.

The VC award ceremony was not the only royal recognition of Thomas's valour: Kenny was invited to the first garden party for VC winners on 26 June 1920 at Buckingham Palace and also to a British Legion dinner held in The House of Lords in 1929 for those who had gained the supreme medal for gallantry.

Here is the citation:

'For most conspicuous bravery and devotion to duty on the night of 4th November, 1915, near La Houssoie. When on patrol in a thick fog with Lieutenant Brown, 13th Battalion, Durham Light Infantry, some Germans, who were lying out in a ditch in front of their parapet, opened fire and shot Lieutenant Brown through both thighs. Private Kenny, although heavily and repeatedly fired upon, crawled about for more than an hour with his wounded officer on his back, trying to find his way through the fog to our trenches. He refused more than once to go on alone, although told by Lieutenant Brown to do so. At last, when utterly exhausted, he came to a ditch which he recognised, placed Lieutenant Brown in it, and went to look for help. He found an officer and a few men of his battalion at a listening post, and after guiding them back, with their assistance Lieutenant Brown was brought in, although the Germans again opened heavy fire with rifles and machine-guns, and threw bombs at 30 yards' distance. Private Kenny's pluck, endurance and devotion to duty were beyond praise.'[5]

The Wheatley Hill Heritage Centre website further adds that:

'A few days later, Thomas Kenny returned home to his wife and family. At the Palace Theatre in Wingate, with the local Boy Scouts and Prize Band as escort and before a capacity audience, he was presented by the Manager of Wingate pit with £50 in War Bonds, a gift from local people.

'The next morning, 11 March, Thomas Kenny went to his old school to be presented with a marble clock, two silver vases and two bronze statues, pipe and tobacco and to listen to a poem specially composed for the occasion and read by one of the children, all of which pupils, parents and teachers had raised money to buy to show their appreciation of Kenny's bravery:

Reception and Presentation
TO
SERGEANT THOMAS KENNY, VC
13th DLI
By the Teachers and Children of Wingate Catholic School,
11 March 1916

Poem written at the request of the children by P. LEAVY
(a resident of Hutton Henry)

Welcome, welcome, once again
Hero brave and bold;
To the school where you were taught,
In the days of old.
We the present pupils,
Of Wingate Catholic School,
Were pleased to hear when death was near
You were so brave and cool

Greater love no man can have
In life; no higher end –
Than that the life God gave to him
He would give for his friend.
And you, a former pupil, of
Our humble Catholic School,
Prepared to make the sacrifice,
Observed the golden rule.

Your deed was not performed,
In the glare of the limelight,
Oh no; you struggled bravely
On a dark and stormy night

'To save your gallant officer –
You did so strive and plan,
The office 'tis truly said
Was worthy of the man

For hours your wounded officer
You carried on your back,
With German snipers following
Close upon your track.
You had the satisfaction,
Tho' his life you could not save,
Of laying the gallant soldier, in
A British soldier's grave.

Upon our Roll of Honour,
We're pleased and proud to see
This day attached to your name
The coveted VC
Your children are our schoolmates,
For you and them we pray;
And ever in our memory, keep
This as a happy day.'

In the evening Thomas Kenny was presented at the Palace Theatre with £50 in War Bonds by the manager of Wingate Colliery; the directors of the Palace added £10 – the proceeds of that night's entertainment.

Thomas Kenny returned to his DLI battalion on the Western Front. October 1916 saw him wounded, but by 1918 he had risen to the rank of Company Sergeant Major. A drift was named in his honour at Wheatley Hill pit – The Kenny Drift. A street in Gilesgate, Durham City was named after him – Kenny Close. In this area of Durham, a number of the streets are named after VC recipients.

Here is how the DLI remembers and honours Thomas Kenny:[6]

'The Thomas Kenny Story'

'When on patrol on 4 November 1915, with Lieutenant Philip Brown, his officer, in No-man's Land, and having lost their way, Lieutenant Brown was shot through the thighs. Under heavy enemy fire Thomas Kenny got Lieutenant Brown onto his back, and struggled for an hour to get back towards the British lines. Having arrived cold, wet and utterly exhausted at a trench he recognised, he made Lieutenant Brown comfortable, and set out to find his battalion's front line. A rescue party was organised, and Thomas Kenny with two stretcher bearers went out again, located Lieutenant Brown and brought him back to British lines. Unfortunately Lieutenant Brown died of his wounds.

'Thomas Kenny was awarded the VC, his citation stating that 'his pluck, endurance and devotion to duty were beyond praise'. His was the first DLI VC of the First World War.

'After the war Thomas Kenny returned to his job as a miner, first at Wingate, then at Wheatley Hill. He died on 29 November 1948 and was buried in Wheatley Hill cemetery.'

'The Inkerman Club Appeal'

'Following an appeal by "The 'Faithful' Inkerman Dinner Club" his unmarked grave was given a headstone in an impressive ceremony held in August 1994, attended by members of the "Faithful" Inkerman Dinner Club, DLI Association branch members and branch standards from throughout the county. His headstone was unveiled by Captain R.W. Annand VC whose VC was the first DLI VC awarded in WW2.'

The VC & GC Association adds that:

'On 4 November 1915, Lieutenant P.A. Brown, 13th Battalion the Durham Light Infantry, was strengthening the British wire at La Houssoie, near Erquinghem, just south-west of Armentières when he was wounded. Private T. Kenny succeeded in bringing him back to the British lines but Brown died shortly afterwards.'[7]

But Thomas Kenny was by no means finished with acts of bravery: during the Battle of the Somme, on 17 July 1916, Thomas saved a Private Frank Moody's life by carrying him to safety after taking a serious gunshot wound to his leg; the leg was subsequently amputated and Moody was discharged in May 1917. Thomas himself was wounded in October 1916 while in 'A' company, but returned to the front and was eventually promoted to Company Sergeant Major. The Division moved east to Italy in November 1917 and remained there for the remainder of the war. Thomas was demobilised in 1919.[8]

Victoria Cross Online continues:

'Post-war, he worked at Wingate Colliery until 1927 and then returned to Wheatley Hill Colliery as a stoneman and drifter. During the Second World War he served in the Home Guard. After an underground shoulder accident in 1944, he became a surface worker.

'Thomas died at South Wingate, County Durham on 29 November 1948 [of natural causes]. He was buried in an unmarked grave in Wheatley Hill Cemetery, until an appeal was launched by members of "The Faithful Inkerman Dinner Club" and a headstone was added in August 1994, unveiled by Captain Richard Annand VC. In addition to his VC, Kenny was awarded the 1914–15 Star, British War Medal 1914–20, Victory Medal 1914–19 and George VI Coronation Medal 1937. His VC is held privately.'

Annand has the honour of being the first VC in the British Army in the Second World War. Richard Annand of Westoe, South Shields, County Durham, was later to become Lord Ashcroft, collector and owner of numerous VCs.

Unfortunately, Kenny's award had no impact whatsoever on Kenny's employment prospects in civilian life. He died on 29 November 1948 at Darlington Street, Wheatley Hill and is buried in the village cemetery.

David Beresford, Kenny's grandson, confirms that reports saying that his grandfather died in a mining accident in 1958 are wrong and that he died of natural causes in 1948.

On 7 November 2015 – nearly 100 years after he saved the life of Lieutenant Brown, a paving stone honouring the life of Thomas Kenny was laid in Wheatley Hill cemetery by the Lord Lieutenant of County Durham. This is one of the paving stones presented to local communities by the Department for Communities and Local Government to commemorate recipients of the Victoria Cross during the First World War. Kenny's was the first of seven stones to be unveiled in County Durham.

The Wheatley Hill History Club concludes by telling us that:

'Launched 9 November 2017 at The Gala Theatre, Durham City – the Thomas Kenny VC film – Beyond Praise.[9]

'This documentary film commissioned by the Wheatley Hill History Club, tells not only his story, but the story of the incredible relationship between Kenny and the man he rescued, Lieutenant Philip Brown. Running time: 1 hour 25 minutes.'

A century after the event, *The Northern Echo* of 4 November 2015 reports that:

'The skies above Wheatley Hill were eerily thick with mist as a trio of buglers from the Durham (The Rifles) Company sounded The Last Post shortly after 11 am.[10] But, as Father Kenneth Crawford, chaplain to the Durham Light Infantry (DLI) Association, reflected, it was misty too at La Houssoie, France, on 4 November 1915 – a day Thomas Kenny, a 33-year-old Private in 13 Service Battalion DLI, would never forget.

'He died on 29 November 1948, aged 66 and was buried at Wheatley Hill Cemetery. Today (Wednesday, 4 November), at that same cemetery, 47 of his descendants were joined by civic and military dignitaries for the unveiling of a commemorative stone honouring his courage.

'Patricia Shaw, Kenny's granddaughter and only surviving relative who can remember him, said: "It's a wonderful tribute. We're absolutely thrilled to bits by it. I'd like to thank everyone who's contributed to it. It's been a really moving day for us".'

William McNally VC, MM and Bar

As we can see 13820 William McNally VC, MM and Bar (16 December 1894 – 5 January 1976) was awarded the VC *and* the MM and Bar – a formidable achievement which reveals consistent bravery of the highest order.

The following biography of McNally is based largely on Roger Chapman's *Beyond their Duty* which commemorates the only occasion on which all 18 Victoria Crosses won by soldiers of the Green Howards regiment came together – April to October 2001, in the Green Howards Museum, Richmond [https://www.ww1-yorkshires.org.uk/vc-winners-yorkshires/html-files/vcgc-mcnally.htm].11

William McNally was born at 12 Bude Square, Murton, near Seaham, County Durham on 16 December 1894. At the age of four, he started at Murton Colliery School, leaving at the age of 14, to follow his father down Murton Colliery (owned by the Seaham Coal Company) as a pit pony boy. Typically for a worker like himself he worked six shifts a week until he was aged 19 years and 9 months when, on 3 September 1914, he enlisted at Sunderland into the Green Howards, committing to three years or for the duration of the war. Records show that he was 5 feet 8 ½ inches tall, weighed 124 lbs, had a fresh complexion, hazel eyes and brown hair.

After basic training he was posted to the 8th (Service) Battalion, the Yorkshire Regiment at Halton Park Camp in Buckinghamshire. William returned home on finishing his training on ten days' leave; home was now 11 Shepperdson Street. On 29 April he was posted as private 13820 to the 11th, then to 'A' company, 10th Battalion Yorkshire Regiment at Aylesbury, then back to Halton Park. After a year's training the Battalion were at Witley Camp by August 1915 before they embarked to Boulogne via Folkstone on 9 September as part of 69 Brigade, 23rd Division; they then headed for their base at St Eloi.[12]

At the Battle of Loos 8th Battalion East Yorkshires and 10th Battalion Yorkshires were to reinforce the units of the 15th division and, if necessary, retake Hill 70. The battalions sustained heavy casualties and William was wounded on 29 September with a gunshot injury to his hand which was treated at 14th General Hospital at Wimereux and then at the Brook War Hospital in Shooters Hill, Woolwich after which he had leave from 19–29 November 1915 which he spent with his family. 12 December saw him posted to the 2nd Battalion, then 'B' Company 8th Battalion after a spell in the 11th.

The decorations started to come on 10 July 1916 when, as a Private, he was awarded his first Military Medal for bravery at Contalmaison during the Battle of the Somme, gazetted on 23 August 1916. He assisted an officer who was wounded in the thigh and hauled him back to safety.

The second MM (i.e. a bar to the first) was won at Passchendaele, recommended on 13 November. Here, on three separate occasions, he rescued men who had been wounded or buried by enemy shellfire. It was finally gazetted on 23 February 1918.

In mid-November 1917, the 8th Yorkshires were posted from the Western Front to northern Italy. Here, 13820 Sergeant William McNally MM carried out three separate acts of gallantry between 27 and 29 October 1918 north east of the River Piave to win the Victoria Cross. The citation was published in *The London Gazette* on 14 December 1918.

Sergeant McNally was 23 years old, and a sergeant in the 8th (S) Battalion, The Yorkshire Regiment (Alexandra, Princess of Wales's Own), when the following deed took place for which he was awarded the VC. The 8th had been picked out for a key role in the crossing of the Piave and began moving into position on the front line on 21 October, where they billeted in farm buildings two miles behind the front, advancing the following day to the left of the front.

The citation reads as follows:

'On 27 October 1918 at Piave River, Italy, when his company was most seriously hindered by machine-gun fire, Sergeant McNally, regardless of personal safety, rushed the machine-gun post single-handed, killing the team and capturing the gun. Later, at Vazzola on 29 October the sergeant crept up to the rear of an enemy post, put the garrison to flight and captured the machine-gun. On the same day, when holding a newly captured ditch, he was strongly counter-attacked from both flanks, but coolly controlling the fire of his party, he frustrated that attack, inflicting heavy casualties on the enemy. Throughout the whole operations his innumerable acts of gallantry set a high example to his men, and his leading was beyond all praise.'[13]

Here is how the Victoria Cross and George Cross Association described his action:[14]

'On 24 October 1918, the final offensive of the Italian campaign, now known as the Battle of Vittorio Veneto, was launched by the Allies on the Piave front. The British were in the centre of the front, north-east of Treviso. On the morning of 27 October 8th Battalion The Yorkshire Regiment took part in the crossing of the Piave, wading through the river from Papadopoli Island, and advancing to Tezze. Sergeant W. McNally distinguished himself by his gallantry in this action. The next day the Yorkshires reached Vazzola and on the 29th crossed the Monticano river on their way to Cimetta. On the far side of the Monticano Sergeant McNally further distinguished himself. In the same offensive Private W. Wood, 10th Battalion The Northumberland Fusiliers, showed conspicuous bravery near Casa Van on the 28th. By this stage, Austria-Hungary was on the verge of internal collapse and an Armistice came into force on 4 November 1918 bringing the war on this front to a close.'

The North East Memorial Project tells how in February 1919, Billy McNally left the army demobilised as a Class Z Reserve at Ripon still plagued by his third wound, a bullet in the leg, but that did not prevent him from returning to work down the mine at Murton Colliery. When he arrived home he was met by a large, enthusiastic crowd including his pregnant wife at the station. He had married Elizabeth Hallimond just before receiving the Victoria Cross in Buckingham Palace from King George V on 17 July 1919. On 11 November 1920 William was part of the VC Guard of Honour for the interment of the Unknown Warrior in Westminster Abbey.

The Tomb of the Unknown Soldier or Warrior

The Tomb of the Unknown Soldier or Warrior is an important monument dedicated to the service of an unknown soldier and to the memories of all soldiers who have perished in war. Throughout history, soldiers have died in war, their remains unidentified. Following the First World War, a movement gathered pace to commemorate these soldiers with a single tomb, containing the body of one such unidentified soldier. In the UK, the Tomb of the Unknown Warrior was established at the Chapel of the Holy in Westminster Abbey, while in France *La tombe du soldat inconnu* was located in the Arc de Triomphe.

The idea was the brainchild of a chaplain at the Front, the Reverend David Railton (1884–1955), when in 1916 he spotted in a back garden at Armentières a grave with a rudimentary cross on which were inscribed the words 'An Unknown British Soldier'. Four years later, he wrote to the Dean of Westminster, Herbert Ryle, through whose efforts this memorial became a reality. The body was selected from unknown British servicemen exhumed from four battle areas, the Aisne, the Somme, Arras and Ypres.

We learn from the Westminster Abbey website that:[15]

'The remains were brought to the chapel at St. Pol on the night of 7th November 1920. The General Officer in charge of troops in

France and Flanders, Brigadier General L.J. Wyatt, with Colonel Gell, went into the chapel alone, where the bodies on stretchers were covered by Union Flags. They had no idea from which area the bodies had come. Brigadier Wyatt selected one and the two officers placed it in a plain coffin and sealed it. The other three bodies were reburied.'

The body of the Unknown Warrior may originate from any of the three services, Army, Navy or Air Force, and from any part of the British Isles, Dominions or Colonies. The tomb represents all those who died who have no other memorial or known grave.

The website continues:

'The next day the coffin was placed inside another which had been sent over specially from England made of two-inch thick oak from a tree which had grown in Hampton Court Palace garden, lined with zinc. It was covered with the flag that David Railton had used as an altar cloth during the War (known as the Ypres or Padre's Flag, which now hangs in St George's Chapel). Within the wrought iron bands of this coffin had been placed a 16th century crusader's sword from the Tower of London collection. The inner coffin shell was made by Walter Jackson of the firm of Ingall, Parsons & Clive Forward at Harrow, north London and the larger coffin was supplied by the undertakers in charge of the arrangements, Nodes & Son.

'The coffin plate bore the inscription:

'A British Warrior who fell in the Great War 1914–1918 for King and Country.

'The ironwork and coffin plate were made by D.J. Williams of the Brunswick Ironworks at Caernarfon in Wales. The destroyer HMS Verdun, whose ship's bell was presented to the Abbey and now hangs near the grave, transported the coffin to Dover and it was then taken by train to Victoria station in London.'

On the morning of 11 November 1920 the coffin was solemnly placed by the bearer party from the 3rd Battalion Coldstream Guards on a gun carriage drawn by six black horses of the Royal Horse Artillery. It then began its journey through the crowded streets, stopping first in Whitehall where the Cenotaph was unveiled by King George V.

At Westminster, after the hymn 'Lead kindly light', the King stepped forward and sprinkled a handful of French earth onto the coffin from a silver shell as it was lowered into the grave. The grave was filled in, using 100 sandbags of earth from the battlefields, on 18 November and then covered by a temporary stone with a gilded inscription on it:

'A BRITISH WARRIOR WHO FELL IN THE GREAT WAR 1914–1918 FOR KING AND COUNTRY. GREATER LOVE HATH NO MAN THAN THIS.'

In 1940 McNally joined his Local Defence Volunteers in Murton as a sergeant, promoted to lieutenant in 1941 as well as serving in the 13th and 16th Battalions of the Durham Home Guard until December 1945. He was a member of the Miners' Lodge Committee and in 1947 became a timber-yard foreman making pit props. On 26 June 1956 he attended the Hyde Park VC Reunion and retired at the age of 65 years in July 1958.

William McNally lived in retirement at 2 Gray Avenue, Murton Colliery for a further sixteen years, taking an active part in the local community and regularly attending VC & GC Association and Green Howard Association reunions. He died at Murton Colliery on 5 January 1976. His ashes were scattered in Sunderland's Garden of Remembrance at the Tyne and Wear Crematorium. In October 1978 his life was commemorated by a stone memorial in Murton Park near the village war memorial. It was unveiled by his widow and their two sons and daughter. Mrs McNally presented her husband's Victoria Cross, Military Medal and Bar, and six medals to the Regiment in 1979.

His VC is displayed at the Green Howards Museum, Richmond, North Yorkshire, alongside the medals of a fellow resident of Murton, James Hall DCM MM.

Wilfred Wood VC

59812 Wilfred Wood was born on 2 February 1897 at 25 Adcroft Street, Stockport. On the death of his father he moved to 52 Chester Road, where his mother remarried and became Mrs Daniels. Norbury Church of England School provided his early education; he was often in the congregation at Norbury Church and was a member of the local football club.

He started his working life in February 1914 on his seventeenth birthday as an engine cleaner at Edgeley shed at Stockport for London & North West Railway. Towards the end of 1916 he enlisted in the Cheshire Regiment as a stretcher-bearer. Training began at Oswestry; he served as a stretcher bearer for the Cheshire Regiment in France before later transferring to the 10th Battalion Northumberland Fusiliers.

Wilfred Wood VC (2 February 1897 – 3 January 1982) was awarded his VC as a 21-year-old in the 10th Northumberland Fusiliers for action during the Battle of Vittorio Veneto. The citation reads:

> 'For most conspicuous bravery and initiative on 28 October 1918, near Casa Van, Italy, when a unit on the right flank having been held up by hostile machine guns and snipers, Pte. Wood, on his own initiative, worked forward with his Lewis gun, enfiladed the enemy machine-gun nest, and caused 140 enemy to surrender.
>
> 'The advance was continued till a hidden machine gun opened fire at point blank range. Without a moment's hesitation Pte. Wood charged the machine gun, firing his Lewis gun from the hip at the same time. He killed the machine-gun crew, and without further orders pushed on and enfiladed a ditch from which three officers and 160 men subsequently surrendered.

'The conspicuous valour and initiative of this gallant soldier in the face of intense rifle and machine-gun fire was beyond all praise.'[16]

The announcement of Wilfred's VC in November 1918, together with the Armistice, caused much joy in Hazel Grove and Bramhall, with brass bands and flags and his fiancée Bessie from Toronto Street on his arm. The official reception was held at Worsley Street Chapel. Local papers covering the event were quick to emphasise the family's community spirit, noting that Wilfred's grandmother had been licensee of the White Hart Hotel for forty years.

After demobilisation the hero returned to Edgeley Shed and became a fireman in 1919. Wood progressed to becoming a driver based at Newton Heath shed in Manchester. Wilfred married Bessie in the same year.

After forty-six years with LNWR he retired in 1960 as a supervisor at Longsight shed. A LNWR Claughton Class locomotive was named after Wilfred in 1922. When this type was withdrawn from service, a London, Midland and Scottish Railway Patriot Class steam locomotive was named after him, from which the nameplate resided at Norbury Primary School in Hazel Grove until it was donated to the Northumberland Fusiliers Museum at Alnwick Castle[17] where other memorials to Wilfred Wood's heroism can be seen, including the brass name plate from 'Patriot' number 5536/45536 that bears his name.[18]

The JD Wetherspoon pub at 204 London Road in Hazel Grove was named after him in 2010. Wilfred Wood had lived at 23 Butley Street in Hazel Grove since 1929.

Wilfred Wood died in Stockport's Stepping Hill Hospital on 3 January 1982 and was cremated at Stockport Crematorium on 8 January, 1982; his ashes were scattered in the First Garden of Remembrance.

For details of the grave locations for holders of the VC in Co. Durham, please visit: https://web.archive.org/web/20041210053045/http://www.homeusers.prestel.co.uk/stewart/codurham.htm

Timeline for Jack Youll VC (1897–1918)

1835 Thornley Colliery established

1881 Northumberland Fusiliers formed in Newcastle-upon-Tyne, 1 January

1882 Triple Alliance (German Empire, the Austro-Hungarian Empire, and the Kingdom of Italy) formed

1897 Jack Youll born in Thornley, Co. Durham, 6 June

1901 Jack attends Thornley Council School; 1911 [?] is a technical student in a class run by Durham County Council at Wingate. 1912 [?] he starts at Thornley Colliery in the power station as an apprentice electrician.

1907 Britain joins France and Russia in the 'Triple Entente'

1914 Gavrilo Princip assassinates Archduke Franz Ferdinand, heir presumptive to the Habsburg throne, and his wife, German-born Sophie, Duchess von Hohenberg, in Sarajevo, Bosnia-Herzegovinia, June 28

1914 July Ultimatum, July 23

1914 A state of war existed between Great Britain from 11.00 pm on 4 August

1914 11th (Service) Battalion formed at Newcastle-upon-Tyne

1914 Princip found guilty of murder and high treason, 28 October

1914 Hartlepool and West Hartlepool, and Whitby and Scarborough bombarded by the German fleet, 16 December

1915 Italy leaves the Triple Alliance for the Triple Entente, May

1915 The Battalion and Division set sail for Boulogne, mustering near Tilques, August

Timeline for Jack Youll VC (1897–1918)

1916	Jack joins the Royal Engineers by way of the 1/1st Durham Field Company or 1st Durham Engineers, a territorial unit, 1 July
1916	JY posted to France as a Royal Engineer, 11 August
1917	JY recommended for officer training; returned to England on 22 February for training
1917	JY gazetted in June as a temporary second lieutenant into the 1st Northumberland Fusiliers before returning to the Western Front in late July, attached to the regiment's 11th Battalion as a temporary second lieutenant
1917	JY mentioned in despatches for valorous action at Polygon Wood, 25 Sept – 3 October 1917
1917	Italians mauled by the Austrians at the Battle of Caporetto, October-November
1917	JY and the 11th Battalion posted to Italy, in response to calls for support from the British and French by the Italians, November
1918	38575 Private Matthew Youll (b.1877) who served with the DLI had been missing since March 1918, later presumed dead.
1918	Princip dies of TB in Theresienstadt, 28 April
1918	Ernest Hemingway and Edward Brittain in the Asiago region; Brittain killed June
1918	Battle of Asiago, 15–23 June
1918	Jack Youll awarded Victoria Cross and Medaglia d'Argento al Valor Militare at Asiago, 15 June
1918	JS returns to Thornley for celebrations to mark his VC and Medaglia d'Argento al Valor Militare, 10 September
1918	Jack Youll killed at Battle of Vittoria Veneto, 27 October during the attack across the River Piave
1918	The Armistice of Villa Giusti ending the war in Italy signed 3 November
1918	Jack's family notified of his death, 10 November
1918	End of the First World War; armistice 11 November
1918	Jack Youll initially buried at Lonadina British Cemetery, Spresiano
1919	He was later reburied at Giavera British Cemetery, June

1997 His medal group, including the VC, British War Medal 1914–20, Victory Medal 1914–19 and Italian Silver Star, sold at Spink for £36,000, December

2005 Memorial erected in Jack's home village of Thornley, County Durham

Appendix 1

The German Bombardment of Hartlepool and West Hartlepool

In the space of forty minutes on the morning of 16 December 1914 about 1,000 shells were unleashed on the towns from the three German heavy cruisers *Blucher*, *Seydlitz* and *Moltke*. The German fleet shelled the towns, killing sixty-three civilians and nine soldiers in Hartlepool and fifty-six civilians in West Hartlepool; 400 or so civilians were injured and much housing stock was damaged or destroyed. Most of the resulting dead were taken to the Public Mortuary in Market Yard, Lynn Street: thirty-five bodies were processed in one day in a building designed to hold four; others were sent to Gray Peverell department store in Victoria Street. The Fire Commander on duty that morning was Lieutenant Colonel L. Robson who successfully retaliated with his own salvoes; he was awarded the DSO and the CMG.

The raid killed the first British soldier to die on British soil in the First World War: Private Theophilus Jones of the 18th Battalion of the Durham Light Infantry, aged twenty-seven. Hartlepool's gun batteries were the only ones in Britain to open fire in anger on the enemy during the First World War.

To the Germans, Hartlepool was a more strategically significant target than Whitby or Scarborough, the other targets that day. It had thriving dockyards and factories, one of which was a converted munitions works and was defended by three BL 6-inch Mk VII naval guns on the seafront – two at Heugh Battery and one at Lighthouse Battery. The guns were manned by the eleven officers and 155 men of the Durham Royal Garrison Artillery.

The Admiralty's response to the bombardment would have done little to calm fears:

> 'Open towns on the East coast must expect to be bombarded and we cannot help it. Those who are killed must be killed and their relatives who mourn must mourn. We are sorry, but this cannot be prevented …we cannot scatter our big ships about to prevent bombardments which, though deplorable, are devoid of military significance.'

King George V, though, sent 'a large number of pheasants' to the homeless, and each wounded person was given a pheasant feather, while the people of Hartlepool camped out in barns away from the shore.[1]

Appendix 2

Other Memorials to Jack Youll

Youll House, Thornley; inscription Second Lieutenant John Youll VC

No longer in use. There were a number of photographs of Jack inside, the location of which is unknown. The building had originally been a colliery hostel and stables around 1914. Formerly used by Age Concern.

The Organ in the Wesleyan Methodist Chapel, Thornley

The new pipe organ was dedicated in September 1923. Inscription: 'To the glory of God and in memory of … who gave their lives in the Great War 1914–1918: "Their name liveth for evermore".' Nine names including Jack Youll.

Book of Remembrance 1961

Now in Thornley Methodist Church, Dunelm Road: 134 names (WW1); 23 names (WW2); 1 name (Northern Ireland)

Appendix 3

Structure of the British Army During the First World War

During the First World War, the British Army was divided into a complicated hierarchical structure of numerous units and sub-units. The structure, down to battalion level, was as follows:

1. General Headquarters/British Expeditionary Force (BEF): FIELD MARSHAL – comprising up to 5 Armies
2. Army (Western Front only; by October 1916 the BEF consisted of the 1st, 2nd, 3rd, 4th and 5th Armies): GENERAL – 2–7 Corps
3. Corps: LIEUTENANT GENERAL – consisted of 2–6 Divisions
4. Division: MAJOR GENERAL – consisted of three or four brigades plus a Pioneer Battalion
5. Brigade: BRIGADIER GENERAL – regiments consisted of two or more battalions; brigades consisted of four or more battalions from different regiments
6. Battalion: LIEUTENANT COLONEL – usually 300–1300 soldiers/4 companies
7. Company: MAJOR – 4 Platoons
8. Platoon: LIEUTENANT or 2ND LIEUTENANT – 4 Sections
9. Section: CORPORAL – 8–14 men

Or, looked at in a slightly different way:

Type	No of Men	Commanded by
Army	40,000+	General
Corps	20,000	Lieutenant General
Division	10–12,000 infantry +6,000 artillery, cavalry, engineers, signallers, logisticians and medics	Major General
Brigade	3–4,000	Brigadier General
Battalion	800–1,000	Lieutenant Colonel
Companies	160–200	Captain or Major
Platoons	40–50	Lieutenant
Sections	10–14	Lance Corporal

Sources: https://www.greatwarforum.org/topic/132099-british-army-structure-in-ww1/
Ball (2016), p. 19

All of the above was subject to considerable variation depending on situations and needs.

Appendix 4

First World War Casualties by Nation

Central Powers	population	mobilised	dead
Austria-Hungary	52m	7.8m	1.2m
Germany	67m	11m	1.8m
Turkey	2.8m	.32m	
Bulgaria		1.2m	0.90m
Allies			
France	36.5m	8.4m	1.4m
Britain	46m	6.2m	0.74m
British Empire		2.7m	0.17m
Russia	164m	12.0m	1.7m
Italy	37m	5.6m	0.46m
USA	93m	4.3m	0.12m

Percentage of total deaths
Entente military 36 per cent
Entente civilians 20 per cent
Central Powers military 22 per cent
Central powers civilians 22 per cent

The total number of military and civilian casualties in the First World War was around 40 million, comprising 20 million deaths and 21 million wounded. The total number of deaths includes 9.7 million military personnel and about 10 million civilians. The Entente Powers (the Allies) lost about 5.7 million soldiers, while the Central Powers lost about 4 million (Source: https://www.census.gov/history/pdf/reperes112018.pdf).

About two-thirds of military deaths in the First World War were in battle, overtaking the conflicts in the nineteenth century when the majority of deaths were due to disease. Nevertheless, disease, including the 1918 flu pandemic and deaths while held as prisoners of war, still caused about one-third of total military deaths for all belligerents.

See Chrystal, Paul, (2023) *A History of the World in 100 Pandemics, Plagues and Epidemics.*

Notes

Preface
1. The Central Powers were one of the two main coalitions that fought in the First World War. They consisted of the German Empire, Austria-Hungary, the Ottoman Empire, and Bulgaria and were also known as the Quadruple Alliance. The Central Powers came about with the alliance of Germany and Austria-Hungary in 1879. Despite having nominally joined this Triple Alliance earlier, Italy did not fight in the First World War on the side of the Central Powers but with the Entente. The Ottoman Empire (late 1914) and Bulgaria (1915) only joined after the start of the War.
2. The Allies, or the Entente, were an international military coalition of countries led by France, the United Kingdom, Russia (withdrew 1917), the United States (joined 1917), Italy, and Japan against the Central Powers of Germany, Austria-Hungary, the Ottoman Empire, and Bulgaria.

Introduction
1. Howard (2002) p. 2.
2. France, Russia, the British Empire, and later Italy (1915) and the United States (from 1917).
3. The incident demonstrates well just how delicately poised relations were at the time. The Agadir Crisis blew up when the French deployed a large number of their troops in the interior of Morocco in July 1911. The reaction of the Germans was to send a gunboat, the SMS *Panther* to Agadir. Germany did not so much object to France's expansion but wanted territorial compensation for itself. Berlin threatened war, sent the gunboat, and stirred up German nationalists. Negotiations between Berlin and Paris resolved the crisis on 4 November 1911: France took over Morocco as a protectorate in exchange for territorial concessions to German Cameroon from the French Congo. See Clark, Christopher, (2013), *The Sleepwalkers*, London, pp. 208–210.
4. Remak, Joachim, (1959), *Sarajevo: The Story of a Political Murder*, Criterion. pp. 137–142.
5. Butcher, (2015), p. 276.
6. Johnson, (1989), pp. 52–54.
7. A formal diplomatic representation (diplomatic correspondence) of the official position, views or wishes on a subject from one government to another government or intergovernmental organization.
8. Howard, (2002), p. 15.
9. Hamilton, Robert, (2015), *Victoria Cross Heroes of World War 1: 628 Extraordinary Stories of Valour*.
10. *See* Chrystal, *Bioterrorism*.

11. Ball, (2016), p. 18.
12. Smith, G.M. (1931), *History of the Great War, Based on Official Documents: Medical Services: Casualties and Medical Statistics of the Great War*, Imperial War Museum.
13. *Op. cit.* pp. 59–64.
14. *Op. cit.* p. 61.
15. *Op. cit.* p. 44–46.
16. *See* Chrystal, *Women at Work*, Chapter 7, for small arms manufacturing.

Chapter 1: Jack Youll (1897–1918) – His Early Life in Thornley, Co. Durham

1. A residential street of twenty-one houses comprising three bedrooms, one bathroom and one reception.
2. See Chrystal, Paul, (2019), *Old Hartlepool and West Hartlepool*, Catrine; Chrystal, Paul, and Laundon, Stan, (2014), *Hartlepool Through the Ages*, Stroud.
3. The Durham Coalfield, Coalmining History Research Centre; 'The Great Northern Coalfield: Mining Collections at Beamish Museum – Northumbria University, Newcastle UK'.
4. See 'The Durham Mining Museum at Murton', http://www.dmm.org.uk/ colliery/m006.htm; Beamish, 'The Living Museum of the North', https://www.beamish.org.uk/.
5. https://web.archive.org/web/20070927005943/; http://www.durham.gov.uk/ miner/projects.nsf/581cd74a9c6aa8b080256d48003758cb/49810d53a07666df80256e8b 003b1a4b? OpenDocument.
6. William Whellan & Co., (1856), *History, Topography and Directory of the County Palatine of Durham*, p. 248.
7. Rymer, Edward A., ed, Neville, R.G., 'The Martyrdom of the Mine or a 60 Years Struggle for Life', in *History Workshop, A Journal of Socialist Historians* (Part 1 Spring 1976) and (Part 2 Autumn 1976). https://wheatley-hill.org.uk/articles/. For more information regarding this industrious and fascinating local history society, see https://wheatley-hill.org.uk/.
8. See Chrystal, Paul, (2022), *Factory Girls: The Working Lives of Women and Children*.
9. For a comprehensive summary of Jack Youll's early life and short but dramatic military career, see Sue Watson's, 'Bravery of Soldiers Won't Be Forgotten', written to commemorate the start of the First World War, *Hartlepool Today*, 6 September 2004.
10. 'The Employees and Residents of Thornley', pp. 9–11.
11. Op. cit. p. 7.
12. Op. cit. p. 10.
13. Op. cit. pp 15–16.
14. Op. cit. p. 25.
15. https://brightonmuseums.org.uk/discovery/history-stories/the-story-behind-the-picture-a-jack-johnson-exploded-near-him/

Chapter 2: Jack Youll and the 1st Durham Engineers

1. Westlake, R.A., (1983), *Royal Engineers (Volunteers) 1859–1908*, Wembley.
2. In 1885. The Suakin Expedition was one of two British-Indian military expeditions, led by Major General Sir Gerald Graham, to Suakin in Sudan, with the objective of destroying the power of the Sudanese military commander Osman Digna and his troops

during the Mahdist War. The first expedition took place in February 1884 and the second in March 1885. Suakin was a red Sea port. Osman Digna (c. 1840–1926) was a follower of Muhammad Ahmad, the self-proclaimed Mahdi in Sudan, and became his best known military commander during the Mahdist War. As the Mahdi's best general, he played an important role in the fate of General Charles George Gordon and the end of Turkish-Egyptian rule in Sudan. In Britain, Osman Digna became a notorious figure, both demonised as a savage and respected as a warrior. Winston Churchill described him as an 'astute' and 'prudent' man, calling him 'the celebrated, and perhaps immortal, Osman Digna'. (Churchill, Winston S., *(1902), The River War: An Account of the Reconquest of the Sudan, p. 47).*
3. The 1st Durham RE (V) sent a detachment of one officer and 25 other ranks to assist the regular REs during the Second Boer War in 1900, and a second section the following year.
4. Major O.M. Short et al, (1933), *The History of the Tyne Electrical Engineers, Royal Engineers, 1884–1933*, Uckfield: Naval & Military.
5. See Appendix 1.
6. Watson & Rinaldi, pp. 62, 69.

Chapter 3: A Very Short History of The Northumberland Fusiliers 1674–1918
1. A hackle is a clipped plume or short spray of coloured feathers that is attached to a military headdress, with different colours being associated with particular regiments. In the British Army and the armies of some Commonwealth countries as well as the Netherlands, US and Swedish armies, the hackle is worn by some infantry regiments, especially fusilier regiments and those with Scottish and Northern Irish origins. The modern hackle has its origins in a much longer plume, originally referred to by its Scots name, *heckle*, which was commonly attached to the feather bonnet worn by Highland regiments (now usually only worn by drummers, pipers and bandsmen). In the case of the Northumberland Fusiliers the hackle is red over white.
2. See Ridge, Robert, (1829), 'Recollections in Quarters: the Affair of El Bondon, 25th September 1811', in *The United Service Magazine*, p. 352; see also Brown, Steve, (2009), [April 2009], *British Regiments and the Men Who Led Them 1793–1815: 5th Regiment of Foot: Northumberland: Major Henry Ridge, The Napoleon Series*; Burnham, Robert, McGuigan, Ron, (2010). *The British Army against Napoleon*, Barnsley.
3. Sergeant (Sgt) is a rank in use by the armed forces of many countries. It is also a police rank in some police services. The alternative spelling, *serjeant*, is used in The Rifles and other units that draw their heritage from the British light infantry. Its origin is the Latin *serviens*, 'one who serves', through the Old French term *serjant*. The term *sergeant* refers to a non-commissioned officer placed above the rank of a corporal, and a police officer immediately below an inspector in the UK.
4. Mallinson, Allan, *The Making of the British Army*, pp. 171–173.
5. In 1958, it had joined the other three English fusilier regiments to form The Fusilier Brigade. Ten years later, in April 1968, these four regiments merged to become The Royal Regiment of Fusiliers. The Northumberland Fusiliers were designated as the new unit's 1st Battalion.
6. Battle Honours: Mons; Marne 1914; Ypres 1914, 1915, 1917, 1918; St Julien; Somme 1916, 1918; Scarpe 1917, 1918; Selle; Piave; Struma; Suvla. Le Cateau; Retreat from

Mons; Aisne 1914, 1918; La Bassée 1914; Messines 1914, 1917, 1918; Armentières 1914; Nonne Bosschen; Gravenstafel; Frezenberg; Bellewaarde; Loos; Albert 1916, 1918; Bazentin; Delville Wood; Pozières; Flers-Courcelette; Morval; Thiepval; Le Transloy; Ancre Heights; Ancre 1916; Arras 1917, 1918; Arleux; Pilckem; Langemarck 1917; Menin Road; Polygon Wood; Broodseinde; Passchendaele; Cambrai 1917, 1918; St Quentin; Bapaume 1918; Rosières; Lys; Estaires; Hazebrouck; Bailleul; Kemmel; Béthune; Scherpenberg; Drocourt Quéant; Hindenburg Line; Epéhy; Canal du Nord; St Quentin Canal; Beaurevoir; Courtrai; Valenciennes; Sambre; France and Flanders 1914–18; Vittorio Veneto; Italy 1917–18; Macedonia 1915–18; Landing at Suvla; Scimitar Hill; Gallipoli 1915; Egypt 1916–17.
7. https://www.nam.ac.uk/explore/royal-northumberland-fusiliers.
8. The Victoria Cross was awarded to:
   1. Lance Corporal Thomas Bryan, 25th Battalion, 9 April 1917, Arras, France
   2. Private Ernest Sykes, 27th Battalion, 19 April 1917, Arras, France
   3. Temporary Second Lieutenant Jack Youll, 1st Battalion attached to 11th Battalion, 15 June 1918, Asiago, Italy
   4. Second Lieutenant James Johnson, 2nd Battalion attached to 36th Battalion, 14 October 1918, Wez Macquart, France
   5. Private Wilfred Wood, 10th Battalion, 28 October 1918, Casa Vana, Italy

Chapter 4: 11th Northumberland Fusiliers in France
1. 4 July 2018 https://www.greatwarforum.org/topic/262436-what-was-a-service-battalion/.

Chapter 5: 11th Northumberland Fusiliers Regimental War Diaries and Orders
1. http://www.greatwar.co.uk/research/military-records/british-army-war-diary.htm#purpose. *War office, Field Service Regulations: Part II*, pp.174–175.
2. W.O. 95/214.
3. A novel method of artillery use evolved during the First World War, commonly called hurricane bombardment. This is a very quick but intense artillery bombardment, in contrast to the prevailing artillery tactic of long bombardments, sometimes lasting days. Various forms of quick bombardments were employed at several times and places during the war, but the most successful use of hurricane bombardment was when it was combined with German infiltration tactics in which local forces take immediate advantage of any enemy weak points they find, as here.
4. So that soldiers in front-line trenches could fire through the parapet, a fire-step was dug into the forward side of the trench. The fire-step was 2 or 3 feet high. It was on this that the sentries stood; it was also used by the whole unit when standing-to in face of an anticipated enemy attack.

Chapter 6: 11th Northumberland Fusiliers: Hill 60 (Ypres) and the Battle of Messines
1. Hill 60 is a local landmark that has special meaning for the residents of Crawcrook, having been used for informal recreation under the Durham Wildlife Trust, and having taken its name from a battle of the First World War in which local men took part while serving with the Northumberland Fusiliers. Crawcrook, Marchetti Muse, Gateshead NE40 4FB. NZ137 630.

2. Hill 60 is a now a First World War battlefield memorial site and park in the Zwarteleen area of Zillebeke south of Ypres, Belgium. It is about 3 miles from the centre of Ypres. Before the First World War the hill somewhat ironically was known locally as *Côte des Amants* (Lover's Knoll). The northern area was known by soldiers as *Hill 60* about 60 feet above sea level, while the southern part was known as *The Caterpillar*. This afforded artillery observers an excellent view of the terrain around Zillebeke and Ypres. Artillery-fire and mine explosions during the war changed the shape of the hill and flattened it considerably. Today the peak of Hill 60 is only about 13 feet higher than the surrounding land. In 1914, Ypres had 2,354 houses and 16,700 inhabitants inside medieval earth ramparts faced with brick and a ditch on the east and south sides. Possession of the higher ground to the south and east of the city gives ample scope for ground observation, enfilade fire and converging artillery fire. An occupier of the ridges also has the advantage that artillery positions and the movement of reinforcements and supplies can be screened from view. The ridge had woods from Wytschaete to Zonnebeke, giving good cover, some of notable size such as Polygon Wood and those later named Battle Wood, Shrewsbury Forest and Sanctuary Wood.
3. Edmonds, J. E.; Wynne, G. C., (1995) [1927], p. 167.
4. Holt and Holt (2004), pp. 229–231.
5. By January 1915 it had become evident to the BEF at the Western Front that the Germans were mining to a planned system. As the British had failed to develop suitable counter-tactics or underground listening devices before the war, Field Marshals French and Kitchener agreed to investigate the suitability of forming British mining units. Following consultations between the Engineer-in-Chief of the BEF, Brigadier George Fowke, and the mining specialist John Norton-Griffiths, the War Office formally approved the tunnelling company scheme on 19 February 1915. Norton-Griffiths ensured that tunnelling companies numbers 170 to 177 were ready for deployment in mid-February 1915.
6. Hussey, A. H.; Inman, D. S., (1921), p. 62.
7. Fuller, S., (2011), *1st Bedfordshires. Part One: Mons to the Somme*, Hitchin: Fighting High, pp. 128–130.
8. Lucas & Schmieschek, (2015), pp. 85–86.
9. Hussey & Inman, (1921), pp. 63–64.
10. Edmonds & Wynne, (1995), pp. 167–170; Lucas & Schmieschek, (2015), p. 86.
11. Edmonds, J. E.; Wynne, G. C., (1995) [1927], p. 60.
12. *Camouflet*: an underground or subsurface explosion of a bomb or shell that leaves a sealed pocket of smoke and gas.
13. Sandilands, pp. 143–146.
14. Sandilands p. 167.
15. Sandilands pp. 166–167.
16. Sandilands pp. 174–175.
17. Sandilands p.175.
18. Howard, (2002), p. 89.
19. *Battle of Polygon Wood*. This booklet is an initiative of the Defence Reserves Association (NSW) Inc. and the Military Police Association of Australia Inc. as part of their Schools Military History Program. Written and compiled by Matt Walsh JP. MLO

ALGA (MCAE) Dip Bus & Corp Law (CPS) © 2008 – Published by Matt Walsh 115 Leacocks Lane Casula 2170.
20. Cave, Nigel, (1998), p.104.
21. Sandilands p. 194.

Chapter 7: 11th Northumberland Fusiliers in Italy and the British Expeditionary Force (Italy)
1. Seth, (1965), p.147.
2. Gooch, (2014), pp. 245–246.
3. Falls, Cyril, (1966), *Caporetto 1917*, Weidenfeld & Nicolson. p. 25.
4. Haber, Leonard, (1986), p. 186.
5. The Livens Projector was a simple mortar-like weapon that could hurl large drums filled with flammable or toxic chemicals.
6. Gudmundsson, Bruce, (1989). *Stormtroop Tactics. Innovation in the German Army, 1914–1918*, Praeger.
7. Macksey, Kenneth, (1997), *Rommel: Battles and Campaigns*, Da Capo Press. pp. 16–21, 224.
8. Sullivan, Brian R., (1994), 'Chapter 4. Caporetto: Causes, Recovery, and Consequences', in Andreopoulos, George J.; Selesky, Harold E., eds., *The Aftermath of Defeat: Societies, Armed Forces, and the Challenge of Recovery*, (New Haven, Connecticut: Yale University Press, p. 60.
9. Schindler, John R., (2001), *Isonzo: The Forgotten Sacrifice of the Great War*, Greenwood p. 263.
10. Tucker, Spencer C., (2010), *Battles That Changed History: An Encyclopedia of World Conflict*. United States, ABC-CLIO, p. 430.
11. Cassar, (1998), p. 232.
12. Marshal of Italy Luigi Cadorna, OSML, OMS, OCI (4 September 1850 – 21 December 1928) was an Italian general, Marshal of Italy and Count, Chief of Staff of the Italian Army from 1914 until 1917.
13. Townley, Edward, (2002); Collier, Martin (ed.)., *Mussolini and Italy*. Heinemann. p. 16; Regan, Geoffrey, *More Military Blunders*, p. 160.
14. Morselli, Mario, (2001), *Caporetto, 1917: Victory Or Defeat?* Routledge, p. 133.
15. Clodfelter, Michael, (2017), *Warfare and Armed Conflicts: A Statistical Encyclopedia of Casualty and Other Figures, 1492–2015*, (4th ed.). Jefferson, NC, p. 419; 'First World War. com – Primary Documents – G.M. Trevelyan on the Battle of the Piave River, 15–22 June 1918'.
16. This is an adapted extract from the Battalion war diary which is held at the Public Record Office, in documents WO95/2182 and WO95/4236. It can also be found at the website of the British Army 1914–1918 *The Long Long Trail*. My thanks to Chris Baker for allowing me to use extracts from his encyclopaedic body of work, particularly in relation to Jack at the Battle of Asiago Plateau, based on the war diaries of the various divisions, along with a mixture of divisional and regimental histories; his website is at https://www.fourteeneighteen.co.uk/chris-baker/
17. Ball, (2016), p. 147.
18. Gladden, (1971), p. 47.

19. *Op.cit.* p. 73.
20. *Op. cit,* pp. 78–79.
21. *Op.cit.* pp.120–121. See also Chrystal, *Women at Work in World Wars I and II, passim.*
22. Gladden, (1971), pp. 122–123.
23. *Op.cit.* p. 128.
24. Byerly, C.R., (2005), *Fever of War. The Influenza Epidemic in the U.S. Army during World War I,* New York.
25. P. Wever and L. Bergen, (2014), 'Death from 1918 pandemic influenza during the First World War: a perspective from personal and anecdotal evidence', *Influenza and Other Respiratory Viruses, Vol.*8, No.5, 1 September 2014, p.539–540.
26. Byerly, C.R., (2005).
27. Sassoon, S., (1937), *Sherston's Progress (the Memoirs of George Sherston #3)* , New York, Doubleday, Doran & Company, p.75, quoted in Coombs, H. G., (2020), 'The Influenza Pandemic of 1918: Military Observations for Today', in Tardy,T., (Ed.), *COVID-19: NATO in the Age of Pandemics,* (pp. 61–70), NATO Defense College.
28. Wever, P. and Bergen, L., *op.cit,* p. 540.
29. Gladden, *op.cit.,* p. 147.

Chapter 8: The Battle of Asiago, 15–23 June
1. Gladden, *op.cit.,* pp. 150–151.
2. https://www.cwgc.org/our-work/blog/an-italian-expedition-commonwealth-troops-at-the-battle-of-piave-river/
3. *'Letter from Harukichi Shimoi'*. Harukichi Shimoi was a professor at the University of Naples. A lover of Dante, he moved to Italy in order to learn Italian so he could read the Divine Comedy in its original language. Stirred by the great patriotic sentiment of pre-war Italy, Shimoi volunteered to join the war effort where he fought bravely. It was during this time that Shimoi introduced Karate to the Italian people.
4. Halsey, Francis Whiting, (1919), *The Literary Digest History of the World War: Compiled from Original and Contemporary Sources,* Funk & Wagnalls Company, V.9, p 143.
5. Rothenburg, G., (1976), *The Army of Francis Joseph,* West Lafayette: Purdue University Press, pp 212, 213.
6. Simonds, Frank Herbert, (1920), *History of the World War, Volume 5,* Doubleday, p 359.
7. Clodfelter, 2017, p. 419.
8. Tucker, Spencer. *World War I: Encyclopedia, Volume 1,* p. 919.
9. Gladden, *op.cit.,* pp. 170.
10. Chrystal, Paul with Major (Retd.) David Chrystal BEM MiD, (2023), *Gunners from the Sky: 1st Air Landing Light Regiment in Italy and at Arnhem, 1942–1944.*

Chapter 9: Jack Youll's VC Action
1. https://www.newmp.org.uk/article.php?categoryid=99&articleid=1375&displayorder=5
2. On https://www.keymilitary.com/article/temporary-second-lieutenant-john-scott-youll
3. Gladden, *op.cit.* pp. 177–78, https://www.flickr.com/ people/illustratedchronicleww1/ Newcastle Libraries adds: 'During the Great War the *Illustrated Chronicle* published photographs of soldiers and sailors from Newcastle and the North East of England, which had been in the news. The photographs were sent in by relatives and give us a

glimpse into the past. The physical collection held by Newcastle Libraries comprises bound volumes of the newspaper from 1910 to 1925. We are keen to find out more about the people in the photographs'. Posted 13 January 2016 by John Dixon: 'Newcastle City Library has just announced: Launching of 11,000 images from the *Illustrated Chronicle* on Flickr. These are images that were sent in to the *Illustrated Chronicle* by family or friends of soldiers or sailors who served in the Great War and were wounded, killed, decorated, or when they enlisted. They are also looking to find some background information to some of the images. The images are searchable by surname – use the magnifying glass at the top right hand side'. Website address is: https://www.flickr.com/photos/ illustratedchronicleww1
4. 'Nel 1 Centenario della istituzione della Medaglia al Valor Militare', edizione del 1933 dell' Ufficio storico dell' esercito.

Chapter 10: The Hero Returns to Thornley, 10 September 1918

1. Third Supplement to *The London Gazette of 23 July 1918*. 25 July 1918, Numb. 30811, pp. 8723–24.
2. VCs awarded:
1854 – 1914	522
1914 – 1918	628
1918 – 1938	11
WWII	183
KOREAN WAR	4
SINCE 1954	16

   See also the VC & GC Association, https://vcgca.org/our-people/profile/729/John-Scott-YOULL
3. See also *The Employees and Residents of Thornley* ..., p. 136.
4. Third Supplement to *The London Gazette* of 9 July 1918. 11 July 1918, Numb. 30790, p. 8155.
5. https://www.cwgc.org/our-work/blog/an-italian-expedition-commonwealth-troops-at-the-battle-of-piave-river/

Chapter 11: Ernest Hemingway and Edward Brittain in Asiago

1. https://www.theworldwar.org/learn/about-wwi/young-mr-hemingway-italy.
2. https://simonjoneshistorian.com/2015/05/17/the-italian-front-in-the-first-world-war-at-asiago-granezza-and-barenthal-road/.
3. © by owner provided at no charge for educational purposes.
4. https://allpoetry.com/Arsiero-Asiago.
5. In *88 poems of Ernest Hemingway*, edited by Nicholas Gerogiannis.
6. The Second Battle of the Piave River, 15–23 June 1918.
7. https://www.greatwarforum.org/topic/71529-hemingways-a-farewell-to-arms-how-true/page/2/.
8. https://www.greatwarforum.org/topic/71529-hemingways-a-farewell-to-arms-how-true/page/2/.
9. https://www.corriere.it/esteri/19_gennaio_21/ritrovato-un-secolo-nome-soldato-italiano-che-salvo-hemingway-ffc67208-1d70-11e9-bb3d-4c552f39c07c.shtml. See also https://www.washingtonpost.com/ outlook/hemingways-world-war-i-savior-is-

anonymous-no-more/ 2019/01/18/d3dbbb32-0ea0-11e9-831f-3aa2c2be4cbd_story.html.
10. Spanier, Sandra (ed), *The Letters of Ernest Hemingway 1907–1922 Vol.I*, Cambridge.
11. 18 January 2019.
12. *The Times*, 21 October 1916, cited in Vera Brittain, (1989), *Testament of Youth*, New York, p. 288.
13. Brittain, Vera, *Testament of Youth*, p. 356.
14. National Archives WO95/4229).
15. https://simonjoneshistorian.com/2015/05/07/where-and-how-did-edward-brittain-die/ – on which much of the preceding information on Edward Brittain is based. Vera Brittain visited Hudson in 1918 and in *Testament of Youth* describes how he told her that her brother was 'sniped' by an Austrian officer and shot through the head, following the counterattack he had just led. She also refers to a letter received from a Private in her brother's company: 'Shortly after the trench was regained Capt. Brittain who was keeping a sharp look out for the enemy was shot through the Head by an enemy sniper, he only lived a few minutes'. Jones adds that the account of the action on San Sisto Ridge is based on Francis MacKay, (2001), *Asiago*, with reference to War Diaries of 11th Battalion Sherwood Foresters (WO95/4240) and General Staff 23rd Division (WO95/4229), plus Percy Fryer, (1920), *The Men from the Greenwood*. Reference to the revelations by Charles Hudson is made by Mark Bostridge, (2014), *Vera Brittain and the First World War*.
16. GRANEZZA BRITISH CEMETERY Plot 1. Row B. Grave 1. 'Son of Thomas Arthur and Edith Mary Brittain, of 10, Oakwood Court, Kensington, London. Edward Brittain was the brother of Vera Brittain, author of "Testament of Youth".' https://www.cwgc.org/find-records/find-war-dead/casualty-details/638748/edward-harold-brittain/

Chapter 12: Jack Youll Killed in Action at the Battle of Vittorio Veneto, October 1918
1. Paoletti, Ciro, (2008), *A Military History of Italy*, Greenwood Publishing Group, p.15.
2. Gerwarth, Robert, (2020), *November 1918: The German Revolution*, Oxford University Press, p. 65; Thompson, Mark, (2009), *The White War: Life and Death on the Italian Front 1915–1919*, Basic Books, p. 363; Arnaldi, Girolamo, (2005), *Italy and Its Invaders*, Harvard University Press, p.194.
3. As part of XIV Corps. XIV Corps was formed in France on 3 January 1916 under Lieutenant General the Earl of Cavan. It took part in the Battle of the Somme in 1916; a year later it fought through the Battle of Passchendaele before being redeployed to Italy in November 1917.
4. https://www.greatwarforum.org/topic/56340-23rd-division%E2%80%99s-activities/.
5. When the battle was fought in November 1918, the nearby city was called simply Vittorio, named in 1866 for Vittorio Emanuele II, monarch from 1861 of the newly created Kingdom of Italy. The engagement, the last major battle in the war (1915–1918) between Italy and Austria-Hungary, was generally referred to as the Battle of Vittorio Veneto, i.e. 'Vittorio in the Veneto region'. The city's name was officially changed to Vittorio Veneto in July 1923.
6. A bund is an embankment or dyke.
7. WO 95/4240.

8. *St George's Gazette*, 30 November 1918.
9. Peter Banyard, 'Vittorio Veneto', *War Monthly*, Issue 31, pp. 37–38.
10. On 29 October the Austro-Hungarian line along the river began to crack. The breakdown of the defence coincided with declarations of independence from the provisional Czechoslovak government in Prague and the Hungarian dissolution of their union with Austria.

    Short of equipment, rations, and manpower, the Austro-Hungarian army was no longer a viable fighting force. Some units simply abandoned their positions and began marching home to their new nation states. From 30 October the Italian advance was slowed only by the burdensome and rapidly growing number of prisoners. On 3 November an armistice was signed, to come into effect on the following day. The Austro-Hungarian command ordered its men to cease hostilities after the signing, but the Italians continued their advance, taking many more prisoners and reaching the Isonzo River without opposition. Losses: Italian, 40,000 casualties; Austro-Hungarian, 30,000–80,000 casualties and some 450,000 captured.
11. For details see https://www.cwgc.org/find-records/find-war-dead/casualty-details/639711/john-scott-youll/ and https://www.cwgc.org/visit-us/find-cemeteries-memorials/cemetery-details/70000/giavera-british-cemetery-arcade/. See also *The Employees and Residents of Thornley...*, p. 166.
12. Tezze is a village in the Province of Treviso, a large town north of Venice. The village is 8 kilometres east of Susegana, a town on the main road some 24 kilometres north of Treviso. The British Military Cemetery lies about 270 metres south of the village of Tezze. The personal inscription on Frank's headstone reads: TO THE MEMORY OF MY DEAR BROTHER "THY WILL BE DONE" FROM WINNIE.
13. For details see https://www.cwgc.org/visit-us/find-cemeteries-memorials/cemetery-details/70200/tezze-british-cemetery6
14. See *The Employees and Residents of Thornley...*, p. 181,
15. *Op. cit*, p. 184.
16. *Op. cit*, p. 195.

Chapter 13: Lord Ashcroft's Hero of the Month
1. Spink and Son Ltd was founded in London in 1666 and has since developed into the world's premier collectables auction house. It specialises in the auctioning and private sales of stamps, coins, banknotes, medals, bonds and shares, autographs, books, wine & spirits and lifestyle collectables. www.spink.com. Spink & Son tell us that:

    'To date we have sold over 45,000 lots at auction for a combined total of over £37 million. Our highest total for a medal sale was on 25 November 2010, which realised £1,539,672.

    'Over the years the Medal Department has set and re-set many Auction World Records, including a 'hat trick' of World Records for a Victoria Cross Group at auction.

    'The VC, DFC Group to Flying Officer Lloyd Allan Trigg, Royal New Zealand Air Force (sold 6 May 1998 for £138,000) The VC, DSO, MC and Bar Group to Major General D.M.W. Beak, South Lancashire Regiment, Late Royal Naval Volunteer

Reserve (sold 5 November 2003 for £178,250) The VC Group to Sergeant N.C. Jackson, Royal Air Force (sold 30 April 2004 for £230,000).

'In total Spink has sold 70 Victoria Crosses at auction (as well as many more by Private Treaty), the highest price being for the Outstanding Second War Bomber Command V.C. Group of Six to Lancaster Pilot Flight Lieutenant W. Reid, Royal Air Force Volunteer Reserve, which sold at auction on 19 November 2009 for £348,000 – the world auction record for a Victoria Cross to a British Recipient'.

Lord Ashcroft KCMG PC is a businessman, philanthropist, author and pollster. Lord Ashcroft's VC and GC collection is on public display at Imperial War Museum, London. For more information, visit: www.iwm.org.uk/heroes. For details about his VC collection, visit: www.lordashcroftmedals.com. For more information on Lord Ashcroft's work, visit: www. lordashcroft.com. Follow him on Twitter: @LordAshcroft.

Chapter 14: Thomas Kenny VC, W. McNally VC and W. Wood VC

1. See Batchelor, Peter; Matson, Christopher, (2011), *The Western Front 1915. VCs of the First World War,* The History Press; Oldfield, Paul, (2015), *Victoria Crosses on the Western Front, April 1915–June 1916,* Barnsley; Whitworth, Alan, (2015), *VCs of the North: Cumbria, Durham & Northumberland,* Barnsley.
2. Wheatley Hill and Wingate are villages close to Thornley; http://wheatleyhillheritagecentre.org.uk/thomaskenny.html, and https:// wheatley-hill.org.uk/the-life-of-thomas-kenny-vc/
3. https://www.cwgc.org/find-records/find-war-dead/casualty-details/58362/philip-anthony-brown/:

    'Lieutenant Anthony Brown, Durham Light Infantry 13th Btn, died November 4 1915.
    'Buried at RATION FARM MILITARY CEMETERY, LA CHAPELLE-D'ARMENTIERES I. F. 5.'3. Son of Anthony and Jane Chalmers Brown, of 'Broomhill', Southend Rd., Beckenham, Kent.
    'Personal Inscription: WRITE ME AS ONE WHO LOVES HIS FELLOW MEN R.I.P.'
4. For a summary of Thomas Kenny's outstanding courage see Sue Watson's 'Bravery of Soldiers Won't Be Forgotten' written to commemorate the start of the First World War, *Hartlepool Today,* 6 September 2004.
5. 'No. 29394', *The London Gazette* (Supplement) . 7 December 1915. p.12281.
6. https://web.archive.org/web/20080719174451/http://www.faithfuldurhams.com/inkerman_t_kenny.htm.
7. https://vcgca.org/our-people/profile/317/Thomas-KENNY.
8. https://victoriacrossonline.co.uk/thomas-kenny-vc/.
9. The film can be viewed via https://www.youtube.com/embed/lYgrCUQz4go. It is based on Shannon, Stephen D., (1998), *Beyond Praise: The Durham Light Infantrymen who were awarded the Victoria Cross,* County Durham Books. See also Brazier, Kevin, *The Complete Victoria Cross: A full Chronological Record of all Holders of Britain's Highest Award for Gallantry.*
10. https://www.thenorthernecho.co.uk/news/13944238.dli-first-world-war-victoria-cross-hero-thomas-kenny-honoured-home-village-wheatley-hill-100-years/.

11. Chapman, R., (2001), *Beyond their Duty: Heroes of the Green Howards*, Friends of the Green Howards.
12. As given by the North East War Memorials Project at https://www.newmp.org.uk/article.php?categoryid=99&articleid=1369&displayorder=18.
13. Second Supplement to *The London Gazette* of 13 December 1918. 14 December 1918, Numb. 31067, p. 14776.
14. https://vcgca.org/our-people/profile/857/William-McNALLY.
15. https://www.westminster-abbey.org/abbey-commemorations/commemorations/unknown-warrior.
16. '*No. 31034*'. *The London Gazette (Supplement)* , *26 November 1918. p. 14040.*
17. 'Locomotives named after Victoria Cross Recipients', *The LMS Patriot Project*, The LMS-Patriot Company Ltd.
18. https://www.warmemorialsonline.org.uk/memorial/266933.
    https://vcgca.org/our-people/profile/317/Thomas-KENNY.
    https://web.archive.org/web/20080719174451/.
    http://www.faithfuldurhams.com/inkerman_t_kenny.
    htttps://web.archive.org/web/20080719174451/.
    http://www.faithfuldurhams.com/inkerman_t_kenny.

Appendix 1: The German Bombardment of Hartlepool & West Hartlepool
1. Much of this was published in my *Old Hartlepool & West Hartlepool*.

Further Reading

Ashcroft, Michael, (2007), *Victoria Cross Heroes*, London
Baker, Chris., 'The Northumberland Fusiliers', *The Long, Long Trail*
Ball, Tony, (2016), *Crossing No Man's Land: Experience and Learning with the Northumberland Fusiliers in the Great War*, Solihull
Barrie, Alexander, (1988), *War Underground – The Tunnellers of the Great War*
Brittain, Vera, (2004 edition), *Testament of Youth: An Autobiographical Study of the Years 1900–1925*, London
Butcher, T., (2015), *The Trigger: Hunting the Assassin Who Brought the World to War*, London
Cannon, Richard, *(1838), Historical Record of the Fifth Regiment of Foot or Northumberland Fusiliers*, London
Cassar, George H., (1998), *The Forgotten Front: The British Campaign in Italy 1917–18*, A&C Black
Cave, Nigel, (1998), *Battleground Europe: Polygon Wood*, Barnsley
Chappell, P.B., 'Northumberland Fusiliers', *The Regimental Warpath 1914–1918*
Chasseaud, Peter, (1991), *Topography of Armageddon: a British Trench Map Atlas of the Western Front, 1914–1918*, Mapbooks
Chrystal, Paul and Laundon, Stan., (2014), *Hartlepool Through the Ages*, Stroud
Chrystal, Paul, (2019), *Old Hartlepool and West Hartlepool*, Catrine
Chrystal, Paul, (2021), *The Place Names of County Durham*, Catrine
Chrystal, Paul, (2021), *The History of the World in 100 Pandemics, Plagues and Epidemics*, Barnsley
Chrystal, Paul, (2022), *Factory Girls: The Working Lives of Women and Children*, Barnsley
Chrystal, Paul, (2023), *Women at Work in World Wars I and II*, Barnsley
Chrystal, Paul, (2025), *The Seaforth Highlanders: Aiding the King*, Barnsley
Cirino (ed), Marc and Ott, Mark P., *Hemingway in Italy: Twenty-First-Century Perspectives*, University of Florida Press
Davis, Will, (2010), *Beneath Hill 60*. Sidney: Vintage Australia
Doyle, Aidan, (2005) *The Great Northern Coalfields: Mining Collections at Beamish Museum*, Northumbria University Press, Newcastle
Durham Mining Museum at Murton http://www.dmm.org.uk/colliery/ *m006.htm;* Beamish, The Living Museum of the North, https://www.beamish.org.uk/
Florczyk, Steven, *Hemingway, the Red Cross, and the Great War*, Kent State University Press
Fordyce, W., (1860/1973), *A History of Coal, Coke, Coalfields and Iron Manufacture in Northern England*
Fynes, R., (1873), *The Miners of Northumberland and Durham*
Garside, W.R., (1972), *The Durham Miners 1919–1960*

Further Reading

Gladden, Norman, (1967), *Ypres 1917*, London
Gladden, Norman, (1971), *Across the Piave 1917–1919*, Ilkley
Gliddon, Gerald, (2005), *The Sideshows. VCs of the First World War*, Stroud
Gooch, John, (2014), *The Italian Army and the First World War*, Cambridge
Haber, Leonard, (1986), *The Poisonous Cloud: Chemical Warfare in the First World War*, Clarendon Press, p. 186
Hemingway, Ernest, (2013 edition), *A Farewell To Arms*, London
Holt, Major & Mrs, (2006), *Ypres & Passchendaele*, Barnsley
Johnson, Lonnie, (1989), *Introducing Austria: A Short History*, Ariadne Press
Jones, Simon, (2010), *Underground Warfare 1914–1918*, Barnsley
Howard, Michael, (2003), *The First World War: A Very Short Introduction*, Oxford
Macdonald, Lyn, (1978), *Passchendaele: The Story of the Third Battle of Ypres 1917*, London
Macdonald, Lyn, *The Roses of No Man's Land*, London
Morselli, M., (2001), *Caporetto 1917: Victory or Defeat?*, Military History and Policy, London
Owen, Richard, *Hemingway in Italy*, Haus/University of Chicago Press
Passingham, I., (1998), *Pillars of Fire: The Battle of Messines Ridge, June 1917*, Stroud
Paul, Steve, (2017), *Hemingway at Eighteen: The Pivotal Year That Launched an American Legend*, Chicago Review Press
Remak, Joachim, (1959), *Sarajevo: The Story of a Political Murder*, Criterion
Sanderson, Rena (ed), *Hemingway's Italy: New Perspectives*, Louisiana State University Press
Sandilands, H.R., *The Fifth in the Great War: A History of the 1st & 2nd Northumberland Fusiliers, 1914–1918*, (Reprinted by Naval & Military Press)
Sill, Michael, (1984), 'E.G. Ravenstein and Coal Miner Migration: East Durham in the Nineteenth Century', in *Durham County Local History Society Bulletin* 32, May 1984, pp.2–23.
Smith, G.M. (1931), *History of the Great War, Based on Official Documents: Medical Services: Casualties and Medical Statistics of the Great War*, Imperial War Museum
Thompson, Mark, (2008), *The White War. Life and Death on the Italian Front, 1915–1919*, London
Van Emden, Richard (ed), (2002), *Last Man Standing: The Memoirs of a Seaforth Highlander during the Great War – Norman Collins*, Pen & Sword, Barnsley
War Office, (1922), *Statistics of the Military Effort of the British Empire During the Great War, 1914–1920*
Webb, S., (1921), *The Story of the Durham Miners: 1662–1921*
Whitworth, Alan, (2015), *VCs of the North: Cumbria, Durham & Northumberland*, Barnsley
Wilson, J., (1907), *A History of the Durham Miners' Association 1870–1904*
Wilks, John; Wilks, Eileen, (1998), *The British Army in Italy 1917–1918*, Barnsley
Wheatley Hill History Club:
'Employees and Residents of Thornley, Ludworth and Wheatley Hill – Their Contributions to the Second World War'
'The Thornley Coal Company – Owners of Thornley, Ludworth and Wheatley Hill Collieries – 1830–1885'
'The Weardale Steel, Coal & Coke Company – Owners of Thornley, Ludworth and Wheatley Hill Collieries 1886–1913'
'The Weardale Steel, Coal & Coke Company – Owners of Thornley, Ludworth and Wheatley Hill Collieries 1813 – 1947'

'The National Coal Board – Owners of Thornley, Ludworth and Wheatley Hill Collieries 1947 – 1955'

'The National Coal Board – Owners of Thornley, Ludworth and Wheatley Hill Collieries 1956 – 1976'

'Around Wheatley Hill', a book of local images

Wheatley Hill History Club and YouTube channel 'Beyond Praise', a documentary-film about the life and times of Thomas Kenny

Index

1st Air Landing Light Regiment RA, 82–3
1/1st Durham Field Company, 18–20, 139

Annand VC, Richard, 127–8
Arditi Corps, 62, 111–12
Ashcroft, Lord, 117, 128
Asiago, xviii, 25, 56, 58, 84, 86, 94, 100, 102–103, 106, 139
   Battle of, x, 31, 57, 74, 79–80, 85, 90–1, 139
Atrocities, British, 54
Atrocities, German, 53–4
Austro-Hungarian Empire, xviii, 138
   casualties, 112
   end of, xix, 81, 105–106

Barney Berriman's Portable Theatre, Thornley, 5
Black Hand, Serbia, xxiii–xxiv, xxvi
'Blighty Wounds', xxxi
Blitz, Hartlepool/West Hartlepool, December 1914, xxii, 19, 141–2
British Army, strength, xxviii
   casualties, xxx–xxxi, 58
Brittain, Edward, xix
   at Asiago, 92–3, 100–102, 104, 139
   death, 103, 139
Brittain, Vera, 93, 100–101, 103
Brodie, Captain Ewen, 1st Queen's Own Cameron Highlanders, 55
Brooke, Rupert, xii, 110–11

Cadorna, General Luigi, Italian Chief of Staff, 61
Caporetto, xxviii, 64, 96, 99
   Battle of, xv, 56–7, 59–60, 111, 139
   casualties, 61–2
   defeat for Italy, 60–2
Chrystal, Gunner Eric, 82–3

Diaz, General Armando, Italian Chief of Staff, xxviii, 61–2, 79–80, 105–107
Drunken British Army behaviour in Italy, 66
Durham Fortress Engineers, 18–20

Ferdinand, Archduke Franz, xxiii
   death of, xxiii–xxvi, 138
Flamethrower (*flammenwerfer*), xxix, 53, 60, 79, 102–103
Fraternisation (alleged) with WAACs in France, 66–8

Gas warfare, xxviii, xxxi, 9, 12, 27, 48–9, 51, 59, 71, 74–6, 102
Gladden, Private Edgar Norman, xi, xix, 45, 63–6, 68, 72–3, 75–6, 82–3, 85–6, 109–10
Grenade, xxiii–xxiv, xxxi, xxxiii, 29–30, 41, 54, 59–60, 103, 111, 121

Hartlepool/West Hartlepool, xviii, xxii, 1–2, 19, 90, 121, 138, 141–2
Hemingway, Ernest, xix, 139
   at Vittorio Veneto, 81, 91
   at Asiago, 92–100
Hill 60 (Ypres), 45–7, 49–50
Hudson VC, Lieutenant Colonel C.E., The Sherwood Foresters, 86–7, 103

Infantry warfare, xxviii–xxx, xxxii
   life expectancy of infantrymen, xxix–xxx
   training, xxxiii

Italy and the Entente, xxvii, 56
   and armistice, 31
   Italian army indiscipline, 64–5

Jack Johnsons, 12
John the Bum, 5
July Crisis, 1914, xxiii
July Ultimatum, 23 July, xxvi, 138

Kenny VC, Thomas, xx, 118–30

Lee Enfield rifle No 1 Mark III; 1907 pattern bayonet, xxxii

Machine Gun Corps, xxxii
Malaria, 27, 106
Maxim machine guns, xxxii, 12, 60
McNally VC, MM and Bar, William, xx, 130–6
Messines, Battle of, 30, 45, 49–51
Mining: Thornley compared with France, 15–17, 29
Mortars, xxxiii, 37, 59–61, 82, 112
Medical services in WWI, xxxi

Nedeljko Čabrinović, xxiii–xxiv
Northumberland Fusiliers 1674–1918, Chapter 3
   1st Btn, 26–7
   2nd Btn, 27
   and campaigns, 26
   and Tunnelling Company, 29, 46
   and Victoria Crosses, 26, 51
   and WWI, 25f
   casualties, 26
Northumberland Fusiliers, 11th Battalion, 21, Chapter 4
   casualties, xxxii, 26, 77–8, 84
   Gladden, Private Norman in, 63, 65–6, 109, 110
   at Hill 60 (Ypres) and the Battle of Messines, Chapter 6, 49
   in Italy, Chapter 7
   at Polygon Wood 1917, 51–2

Regimental War Diaries and Orders, Chapter 5
Third Battle of Piave, 84
   at Vittorio Veneto, 107
weaponry, xxxii–xxxiii

Owen, Wilfred, 76

Piave River, xxviii, 31, 57–61, 79–81, 84, 87–8, 94, 96, 99–100, 105–107, 109, 111–12, 114, 131–2, 139
Polygon Wood, xix, 25, 30, 51–4, 90, 139
Princip, Gavrilo, xxiii–xxiv
   arrest and trial, xxvi
   imprisonment and death, xxvi
Psychological trauma (PTSD), xxxii, 26

Rommel, Erwin, 60, 91, 94

Salandra, Antonio, xxvii
Sarajevo, xix, xxiii, 138
Serbia, xxiii, xxv–xxvi, 56
Serbian army, xxiii–xxiv
Sophie, Duchess von Hohenberg, xxiii
   death of, xxiv–xxv
   burial, xxvi
Spanish Flu (H1N1 influenza A virus) pandemic 1918–20, 69–71, 106
   casualties, 70
   Siegfried Sassoon on, 71
   Norman Gladden on, 72
Spink, 110, 113, 117, 140
Stormtroopers and infiltration tactics, 59–60, 63, 102–103

Temperini, Fedele, 99–100
Thornley, 3–4, 114–15
   and casualties, 8–9, 13
   and coal, 2–4
   and Jack Youll, 1ff
   and the mine, 7
   and recruitment, 8
   and women, 7
   and WWI, 7–8
Thornley War Relief Committee, 13

Thornley Workmen's Soldiers and Sailors Help Fund, 114–15
Tomb of the Unknown Soldier or Warrior, 133–5
Treaty of London 1839, xxvii
Trench warfare, xxix, 13–14, 30, 74
Triple Entente, xxii, 138
Tunnelling Companies, Royal Engineers (RE), 29, 46
173rd Tunnelling Company, 46–7
Australian, 50

USA enters war, 68, 93

Vickers machine guns, xxxii, 37, 40
Vittorio Veneto, Battle of, xvi, 25, 31, 81, 94, 99, 105–107, 111, 113, 132, 136

Webb, Sidney, 7
Wood VC, Wilfred, xx, 132, 136–7
World War I, causes of, xxv, xxvii
casualties, 48, 51, 112
impact on Thornley, 7–8, 10–11, Chapter 10, 114–15
end of, Chapter 12
Armistice, 111–14

Youens VC, Second Lieutenant Frederick, 51, 55
Youll VC, Jack, xxix, 7, 31, 33
early life, Chapter 1
his life expectancy in WWI, xxx
military training, xxxiii, 21
weaponry, xxxii, xxxiii
with 1/1st Durham Field Company/ Durham Fortress Engineers, 18–21
and award of Mention in Despatches at Polygon Wood, 53
awarded VC, 77–8, Chapter 9
awarded Italian Silver Medal of Military Valour and Star (Medaglia d'Argento al Valor Militare) by the King of Italy, Victor Emmanuel III, 84, 91
recommended for a Military Cross, 90
returns to Thornley, 10 September 1918, Chapter 10
killed in action, Chapter 12, 114
commemoration, 115
medal set, 117
burial, 117
Youll, Margaret, 1–2, 116
Youll, Private Matthew, 115
Youll, Richard, 1, 9, 116

Dear Reader,

We hope you have enjoyed this book, but why not share your views on social media? You can also follow our pages to see more about our other products: facebook.com/penandswordbooks or follow us on X @penswordbooks

You can also view our products at www.pen-and-sword.co.uk (UK and ROW) or www.penandswordbooks.com (North America).

To keep up to date with our latest releases and online catalogues, please sign up to our newsletter at: www.pen-and-sword.co.uk/newsletter

If you would like a printed catalogue with our latest books, then please email: enquiries@pen-and-sword.co.uk or telephone: 01226 734555 (UK and ROW) or email: uspen-and-sword@casematepublishers.com or telephone: (610) 853-9131 (North America).

We respect your privacy and we will only use personal information to send you information about our products.

Thank you!